WILLIAM SMITH

WILLIAM SMITH
POTTER AND FARMER:
1790–1858

George Sturt

Caliban Books

© Caliban Books 1978

This edition first published 1978
by Caliban Books
13 The Dock, Firle, Sussex, BN8 6NY.

ISBN 090457 3087

This edition is a facsimile of the original published in 1919 under Sturt's pseudonym, George Bourne.

PREFACE

The narrative of the life of my grandfather William Smith, making up the second part of this volume, has been put together from memoranda of the talk of his daughter Ann and his son John. That everything they told me was strictly accurate is not to be pretended, and in fact I have come upon more than one obvious error; but certainly they thought they were telling the truth. And that is also the case with my memoranda of what they said. It is many years ago now that I began jotting down their talk, usually within a few hours of my hearing it; and I am fairly satisfied that the notes compiled here are substantially the product of memories much older than my own.

My own, recorded in Part I. as a setting for the other, are probably of small interest save to myself and the few who share them with me. Yet to me they mean so much I should not know what to cut out even if I tried, although I have been assured too many details have been set down. And I own to indulging a different view of their value. Street Farm, in short, with all its appointments, begins to look like a bit of antiquity of which every memory should be preserved. I think it had been but little altered between Farmer Smith's death and my own visits; it was only a degree quieter, more orderly, more peaceful. And so I was privileged to find there a life quite out of date now: life as it seemed good to the English as long ago as Cowper or earlier—for William Smith was old-fashioned even in his own day; a life, in fact, rapidly vanishing in these unquiet times.

Unquiet. It is largely a question of environ-

PREFACE

ment. In our newer days the English have to learn how they may live with steam and electricity, with wireless and daily papers and the swift movements of cosmopolitan thought—an environment bound to produce unrest and discontent until, after many generations perhaps, a comfortable way of living in it has been found. It is an environment not exclusively English but universal: to fit ourselves to it we must be citizens of the world in temper at least, realizing that the local skills and fitnesses no longer suffice.

But in William Smith's time, as the environment —the heaths and woodland, the animals, the village thought—was so much simpler, so too some social fitness to it had long been achieved, and work in it was satisfying and often delightful, thanks to the old crafts. The rewards of labour were immediate; leisure, in the modern sense, was unknown and unwished for; there was no great provocation to "unrest," at least in country places. By being provincial a man could feel indeed at home and at peace. To know the neighbourhood through and through—this was the way to live. Universal law none knew: a parish of England and the time-honoured habits of English country folk made up the environment. As yet we get nothing like so near and dear to us as that seems to have become to our grandparents. If we are winning the Cosmos we are losing touch with England. Ours is the larger hope, of course, and will lead to the more splendid peace by and by. Meanwhile I seem to have seen, at Street Farm, glimpses of an earlier kind of peace, and I am loath to let slip any detail now.

GEORGE BOURNE.

July, 1919.

CONTENTS

PART I

PART II

CONTENTS

LIST OF ILLUSTRATIONS

WILLIAM SMITH

PART I

CHAPTER I

FARNBOROUGH

THE Farnborough of these pages is a village in an oasis—a bit of rural England—which of old lay half isolated in the wide heaths of Hampshire and Surrey. Modern England has broken up the heaths: their desolation has gone; their silence, their savagery, their impressive beauty; but the change had scarcely begun to tell on them fifty years ago. As late as 1870 or thereabouts they stretched, almost unbroken, east to west from Woking to Heath End beyond Aldershot; and, north to south, from Hartford Bridge Flats to Hindhead. A great road—a "turnpike" out of London—the road to Winchester and South-ampton, entered the solitudes near Bagshot Heath and crossed careless of villages; the Basingstoke Canal gave further access to London; two rail-ways—the South-Eastern and the South-Western —were already bringing modernity; yet still, along the trickling heath streams, the little specks of

green fertility remained almost untouched—speci-
mens of the England Cowper had known, Nelson
had fought for. Every speck, perhaps, had its
village or hamlet; but of them all few can have
been lovelier than Farnborough as I remember it.

But these details had no interest to me, as a little
boy of four or five years old. My memory of Farnborough begins rather with an annual drive—a
Christmas drive in a cab sent by one Compton,
landlord of the Alma at Farnborough—a drive that
began prosaically enough, but ended always in the
land of legend. How the driver, benumbed from
his seven-mile journey, enjoyed a nip of neat gin
before turning back again—this I dimly recall as
an odd fact in natural history; but of the first four
miles or so no hint remains in my memory. We
passed Aldershot, passed Laffan's Plain, without
noticing them. Interest revived enough to leave
me with a faint recollection of crossing the bridge
over the canal—"The Barge River"—but it isn't
an attractive picture I can reconstruct: a stretch
of bleak road desecrated with shanties—shanties
new yet already shabby—shoved up in a hurry to
catch the untidy crumbs of the new trade with
Aldershot. All this had to be left behind, the
Queen's Hotel and all signs of newness left behind,
before the glamour of that drive could begin. But
when it did begin it left an ineffaceable memory.
In the five miles of travel I seem to have slipped

back a hundred years in time—before Aldershot Camp was thought of, or a railway, or anything newer than "The Turnpike."

Farnborough Park, now broken up into "residential" building estates and with many of its venerable trees cut down, gave the first touch. Bitter wintry weather seems connected with it, with deep snow on the roads, on the belt of evergreens that hid the park within an ancient park-paling. The said paling had open squares at the top, worth watching from the cab window; but there, and all overhead, and between the evergreens and the tree-tops, was gloom of dark winter.

By and by, across the road, the Tumble-down-Dick was passed; and soon after it the South-Western Railway station; and then the turnpike was left, for a narrow tree-sheltered by-lane leading to Farnborough.

On the left hand lay Farnborough Hill, still at that time owned by the Longmans; but a little way down the lane, on the right hand, an old field-gate had to be watched for, a witch without a head having been known to sit there o' nights; and from here the distance was measurable, even to a small memory, as only a few minutes farther to Street Farm, Farnborough, the destination of the cab and the very home of bliss.

Soon indeed the "feel" of it begins; for in fact there are the premises opening out on the right hand. All is on that side. First an ancient pottery —"The Potshop"; then a short bit of field. Then cowstalls, a barn, stables; and joining them, where the lane has reached the village and goes no farther, the long low building of Street Farm itself.

Long, low, half-timbered, it seemed to stand right across the village "street," blocking the way there. In fact the village road, narrowing just there, wound away, in the shape of a reaping-hook, past a little orchard patch at the far end of the farm; but this mattered little to me. Of course I couldn't help noticing how, in the other direction, the village street—the handle of the reaping-hook —spread before the farm for a furlong maybe, until the South-Eastern Railway station seemed to close it at that end too. This was too obvious to be missed, as was also "The Old Pollard"—a very ancient elm-tree — standing right out into the "street" near the front of the farm.* Yet nothing of this was of any importance — it was of no importance that several red-brick cottages had been put up near the station. Certainly, I re-member how ugly they looked, how inappropriate, even to my childish eyes. Still they were far enough off to be ignored. They didn't matter. Nothing on earth was worthy of attention save the Farmhouse.

* This venerable tree was removed by the Farnborough Urban District Council in 1917.

CHAPTER II

THE FARMHOUSE

A THREE-FOOT hedge, and behind it a narrow garden, separated the village street from the farmhouse. Very simple was the design of that old, half-timbered, comfortable-looking building. Four rooms in a row made the ground floor—namely, dairy, kitchen, sitting-room, and shop; and atop of these were four bedrooms, of course also in a row. So at least it seemed at first glance. Nor indeed was there any real complication. Only, the dairy had a scullery behind it; and these two, with the large kitchen, made a rather wider — or say deeper — block from front to back than the rest of the house. They jutted forward nearer to the road: the façade of the house had a corner in it; the front of shop and sitting-room was as it were enfiladed from the kitchen entrance. If you came in that way from the village street—through the wicket in the hedge and across the iron-stoned garden path—then you went a little to the right of the sitting-room window and right-turned into the projecting corner of the kitchen. There was no other publicly recognized way into the house.

Mere customers to the shop slanted off to the left
when they had opened the gate from the road.
There was no door opening from outside into the
sitting-room, the window of which, however, com-
manded the approaches on either hand—to kitchen
and to shop—and gave the occupants their clearest
outlook all down the village street. This was the
only window in the building with oblong panes in
the lead-light casements. All the other casements,
long and low, had small diamond panes and were
sufficiently draughty.

The whole inside of the farmhouse seems, to my
memory, packed with details exciting to the sentiment of ancient English peace, order, industry,
simplicity, rustic plenty; yet the source of this
eludes me, when I think of these details. Was it
in the smell of turf fires, or in the shape and black-
ness of the great open hearth in the kitchen, where
turf was almost always burning? Was it in the
sides of bacon, all brown and salted, hanging on
the wall opposite the kitchen hearth? Or in the
clean whitewash of the walls? Or did the sentiment of tranquil plenty steal out, with the smell
of cheeses and of seeds, from that inner portion of
the kitchen, which had been partitioned off to make
a sort of office for the farmer? Sometimes I
wonder if it was the ancient woodwork which smelt
so homely, made one feel so snug. The floors—oak
I think, but perhaps elm—were clean-scrubbed, un-

carpeted, and dark with age, and it may have been from them that I derived, all unawares, such an impression of ancient peace. Or again it may have come from the old dresser the door opened upon— the unpainted dresser that stood under the long window and made such a pleasant place for a spoilt child to play on.

It had no tier of upper shelves, this dresser. Another one had, opposite to it, at the dark end of the room; but this nearer one stood flat-topped— a sort of bench with drawers in it—three brass-handled drawers containing only tablecloths and uninteresting things like that. In the mornings milk was served from there to various callers, after which the slopped milk had to be scrupulously scrubbed away. So, in the course of many years, the softer parts of the grain had been worn down, leaving the harder ribs—an orange-red colour— standing up in close corrugation. I fancy that bare wood of the dresser had its grateful effect on me, so comely it was. There was special joy in clambering on to the bench and sitting there against the window. Outside lay the road by which the cab had come; across the road was a corner house under stately trees; away to the right of them stood the Old Pollard; between corner house and pollard could be seen the quiet village life of the "street," good to watch at all times, and provocative of who knows what childish dreams.

Yet I begin to think the sentiment of those dreams arose from the life within the farm, and especially within the kitchen, after all. If, sitting on the dresser, you turned round with your back to the window to look across the kitchen, you had on your right the row of bacon sides; and opposite them, to the left, beyond street door and door into the sitting-room, first there was an antique armchair and then the wide hearth for the turf fires. Sometimes, by the way—but it was always a nuisance— a guard stood before the fire, objectionable if steaming dishcloths hung over it, and only tolerable because of its upright bars. One of these bars was bent and could be worked round and round like a drill; the whole array of bars lent useful help to the fancy if one wanted to be a lion in a cage.

But there, past the hearth on one hand and the bacon on the other hand, was that darker end of the kitchen with the other dresser already spoken of. I didn't like that dresser, at any rate at night. Cumbered as it was with plates and dishes, a lamp, and other merely useful things, it never lent itself to play; and that wasn't the worst. Somehow it seemed to frown upon children, like the dark end of the room it stood in. Moreover—and this was what I liked least of all—near the end of it, away from the fire, a door opened into the scullery. There was a gloomy staircase in that scullery—bad even by candlelight at bedtime when an aunt guarded one—but alone there, in the dark, a horrible thing. And then, besides the ghostly staircase in the Unknown, the scullery had a back door opening on to the night itself. All this one felt, with a sort of dread, to be associated with the gloomy dresser; and there is no doubt about it, I didn't like it at all. I seldom went to that end of the kitchen, to stay there. I don't remember ever finding myself there, at night time. After dark, when a candle had been lit, and curtains drawn over the window—green chintz curtains—the other end was comparatively snug. It's true, I used to wish no senior would ever draw aside a curtain to let in night—for what cared I for stars?—but on the whole this was no real trouble. But that dark end of the kitchen, with its way out to the back door and silence—oh, it was uncanny.

For often after candlelight and when the curtains had been drawn the back door outside in the dark would set up a weird and dismal creaking on its hinges. I have since been told that it did so always, by day as well as by night, and that pains were taken at times, yet taken in vain, to silence that creepy sound. But in my memory it only occurred at night. A shuffling of footsteps followed it, and one watched to see when the door in the dim corner of the kitchen opened and a man came in, wearing an old-fashioned smock frock and carrying a lantern. The apparition of his coming, it may well have been, woke up in me the feeling of something very antiquated in the whole situation.

Who was the man? Presumably an uncle from the cowstalls, smelling probably of milk and of cattle. I don't recall ever being afraid of him, once he had fairly come in; yet I never got quite used to his coming. And though he cannot himself have been at all an old man, the impression of antiquity about his arrival was strong enough to remain with me to this day. It was old enough to be unfamiliar. Englishmen with lanterns, wearing smock frocks, had been doing just that sort of thing for hundreds of years. Just so, long before Shakespeare's time (not that I had ever heard of Shakespeare then), countrymen had been wont to come shuffling into dim candle-lit farm kitchens, bringing an odour of cowstalls with them. Shakespeare? It might have happened in Harold's time. Old England in person, busy, countrified, kindly, and old as the hills, had entered after the door had given its creaking signal. And that is, I fancy, the spirit that gave such memorable romance to the whole kitchen, in my childish fancy. No doubt the other things helped: the long and curtained window casement, the dresser and the bacon, the turf fires, the old woodwork. A medieval touch came, perhaps, from the village and the roadway.

But it was all focussed, it all received an intensity of life—ancient, undying English life—from the creaking entry of the Man with the Lantern.

The Sitting-Room

To the right-hand side of the entrance or corner door in the kitchen, which for its own part opened upon the courtyard and the street, in the same wall as that and, like that, covered with thick black paint, another latch door led down a step into the sitting-room; and here one came by some centuries nearer to modern times—as near as Cowper at least. Demure, carpeted with a brown-coloured carpet, very quiet, this was no room for childish wintertime romping and has therefore left no very clear impression on my memory. Solid Chippendale chairs gave a pleasant note, and tables shining with elbow-grease. On a high mantelpiece, over a "register" grate, were three or four pieces of "Wedgwood," besides a couple of letter-racks. I think a table with flaps stood against the length of wall under the window; in the window ledge was a china bowl. And right across the room, opposite the window, a double door, with glass in the upper halves, opened upon a little quiet orchard plat at the back of the farmhouse.

On one side of this double door—the right-hand side if you were looking out towards the orchard—a square recess in the wall contained an old drawing (the portrait of my great-grandmother) behind a row of china cups, and under this recess was a narrow table with three or four books piled on it. I found, when I was able to read, an early volume of the *Day of Rest* there, with fascinating pages about the stars by Proctor.

The opposite corner—between the double doors and the fireplace—was partitioned off by a square cupboard, not beautiful but doubtless useful. Sometimes I saw it opened, yet what it contained I hardly remember. A faint smell of spices came from it; there were bundles of little brushes for black-leading; but the only thing I really cared for in it was a wonderful toy brought out to amuse me—a Hessian soldier on a horse that solemnly pranced, its front legs pawing the air, its hind hoofs balanced in a little grooved scaffolding designed for just that purpose. As the horse pawed up and down, thanks to the momentum of a curved weight descending from his belly between the two uprights of his perch, his rider, red-coated and with three-cornered hat, solemnly turned his head from side to side. Such a vacuous face I have seldom seen; but to me he was worth all the rest of that cupboard put together. Moreover, he gave the period. He was eighteenth century.

Along the wall opposite to the firegrate, and standing so that the door from the kitchen opened against the head of it, was a sofa covered with shiny

THE TOY HORSE SOLDIER

black horsehair, as was also a stiff bolster which lay in the angle of it. Lying on the sofa—it was a bit slippery—and looking towards the fire, one saw pleasing reflected lights on the intervening table. Not so pleasing—and it seemed to last out over a long period—was a noisome stench that once pervaded the precincts of the sofa, and was traced at last to a dead rat that had fallen down behind the wainscot. An odd thing is that I cannot remember the wainscot, so I incline to think the walls must have been papered. But this is only surmise. It is not memory.

On Sundays and special occasions we used to have tea in this sitting-room. The round table was covered with a white cloth and heaped up with good country food: home-made butter and home-made bread, "lardy'" cake, and a rich plumcake with lemonpeel in it—not very nice, to my taste. Nor was I too appreciative of the cream in the tea instead of milk.

Although by no means tied to one place, the grey-haired Grandmother of the farm—Susannah Smith, its owner since her husband's death many years previously—seemed to have her special sanctum in this sitting-room. Here, I think, the lamps were brought o' mornings for her to clean; here my memory sees her sitting near the fire, a revered and genial old person, in her high-backed shapely armed Chippendale chair. She had a habit, if she sat inactive, of rubbing her fingers briskly over the edge of the tablecloth, or over her own black silk apron (or "apern"), and I daresay her thoughts went the more smoothly to this accompaniment. Anyhow, I am glad to have seen it, in view of an anecdote that will have to be told.

At the round table in the middle of the sitting-room the Grandmother used to sit down to accounts with her eldest daughter—another Susanna Smith. It was probably the most primitive book-keeping —making up bills to the villagers for milk, bread, bacon, or what not; and it is likely that the writing was all done by the Grandmother, while her daughter sat by dictating. Certainly I have no proof of this; only I know that the daughter had had only the scantiest schooling, and I have a dim memory of two women sitting at a table, amidst a shuffling of papers and with an occasional glitter of spectacles. The whole scene is good-tempered, a bit humorous perhaps, but eminently practical; and somebody's voice is reading out, for somebody else to enter in a book, the names of village people now long dead. Even from my memory the last echo of it might as well be gone: nothing remains of it but the faintest suggestion of a monotone. Such as it is, however, this echo must have been started (I make no doubt of it) fifty years ago or so, by the quiet voice of Aunt Susan, engaged in one of her hundred and one duties in the old farm.

This brings me to the shop—Aunt Susan's shop; and yet, before leaving the sitting-room, I must point to the narrow folding table that stood under the long street window. For there, long afterwards, when I was old enough to sit up as late as the others, I saw the careful erecting of a curious pile of chairs on this table under the window. The idea was to set it up so that it could not fail to come down with a great clattering that would rouse the house if any burglar should try to get in at the window. We used to smile at this as at an old lady's whim; yet I perceive there may be some history in it: it may date from ancient scares over the Machinery Riots. Whim or no, the idea was always carefully carried out. It was the Grandmother's last precaution before going upstairs to bed.

The Shop

On the other side of the wall behind the sitting-room fireplace lay the last room on the ground floor—a room much like the sitting-room itself—that is to say, with a window facing the street and so stretching ten or twelve feet back to double glass doors that opened (though I never saw them opened) upon the little shut-in orchard at the rear. But this, in my memory, was never anything but a little tranquil old-fashioned village shop. It had a pleasant odour of groceries, yet grocery was not all it held. In the window were delectable glass

jars containing sweets—acid-drops, pear-drops—
good to see even if one didn't come in for a small
gift of these "lollipops." A string-bag, full of
whitish halfpenny balls, hung from a ceiling rafter,
alongside of the bunches of tallow candles and of
brushes. But things to eat made up most of the
stock-in-trade.

To get from the kitchen to the shop you had to
go across under the sitting-room window to an
opposite latch door—black-painted like the others
—then through a three-foot lobby; and there you
were, plump in amongst the customers (if there
were any)—and faced by a wooden counter, with
scales, biscuit-tins, loaves and other odd things on
it. This was on your left hand, if you were a
customer and walked straight in from the street.
The street door beside the shop window—the door
under the legend "Susanna Smith, licensed to sell
Tea, Coffee, Tobacco, Snuff, Vinegar, and Soap"—
would have it so; and the shopkeeper coming from
her own sitting-room had to go down the length
of her shop almost to the end before she could get
in behind her own counter. But what a place to
get to! What joy to explore those fascinating
drawers! One drawer in particular I remember,
because the caraway-seed in it was so dainty and
sweet-smelling, and the tiny scoop for the seed such
a neat little toy of a thing.

Another toy by the way (or so I used it) was a

diminutive coffee-mill. By standing on the old portable wooden steps—two steps—meant for enabling grown-up people to touch the ceiling, a child could just reach the coffee-mill. It was bolted or screwed to a post at the far end of the counter; a tin cup more than filled the "hopper" of it with coffee beans; another tin, hung to the post by a string which had turned rich brown with the dust, received the grindings from the shoot. And nothing can express the satisfaction one had from the fragrance, the low sound of the grinding, the "feel" as one turned the handle, and, perhaps, the virtuous sense of being at a useful grown-up task for once. On the floor, below the coffee-mill, was a bin to hold flour; but the floor used to clog the scoop, which moreover was a big clumsy thing not to be compared to the scoop in the caraway-seed drawer. It had the same shape, and that was its one attraction. As a plaything it had no charm.

Was there anything else in the shop worth attention? I recall a bench opposite the counter, with butter, lard, bread, chunks of bacon—products, all of them, of the farm; and, by listening, I can almost cheat myself into a fancy that I have heard the shop-bell again on the street door and that a village customer has come in. But this is at least half a cheat. I have no real memory of these details. If they are worth recalling now, it is because, without doubt, their presence was helping to build up

in me, with unnoticed touches, a feeling I should be
very sorry to lose now—a feeling, however ridiculous, that in my childhood I looked upon England
a hundred years ago and more, an England going
strong then with vigorous country life.

The Scullery and the Dairy

I have left this other end of the farmhouse alone,
because my memories of it are so scanty and, at
best, can hardly belong to the winter, or be so snug
as those of the adjacent kitchen. As has been
already intimated, on arrival in the cab the dairy
window was the first to be reached. But it was the
last, if approached indoors. From the shop the
way to it was through the sitting-room, again to
the kitchen, and then diagonally across to the partition door in the darker corner of the kitchen.
Then that door being opened there was the scullery.

The creaking back door to the outer world stood
at right angles to you, on the left. It had a roller
towel on it. Next, was a window—diamond-
paned—giving upon the farmyard. A pump—with
sink under the window—came next. Behind the
pump, and facing anyone coming in from the
kitchen, was the brown-stained staircase mentioned
some pages back. Though not ghost-haunted, it
ought to have been, it was so dark. It filled all
that side of the scullery.

The remaining side—the fourth side—had two

doors in it. One—I never saw it open more than once or twice—gave access to a gruesome black pit, the cellar, which I had no wish to explore. The other doorway led, down a step, into the dairy.

Immediately opposite to the door in the dairy was the window which the cab had passed. Insignificant then, it seemed little better from the inside. All a child could see from it, standing on the low bricked floor, was the ivy ringing it round, and the light was uniformly subdued; and so was the temperature. It may have been the coolness, the quiet cleanness, of the place that kept me away from it. More likely my elders kept me away, to save me from dipping a finger into any of the shallow pans for collecting cream that stood all round. On low slabs, and well within reach therefore, these pans were almost irresistible. About fifteen inches across—they were an old-fashioned red earthenware, of course from the adjacent pottery. I didn't think of that. Nor did I consider that higher shelves may have been used as a larder. All I thought of was the cream: and I knew little about even that. Somehow, it wasn't very often I found myself in the dairy.

Upstairs

I have mentioned the staircase in the scullery—that gloomy staircase so creepy to go up, even by candlelight and even with a mother or an aunt to

take care of one.   At the very end of the house it
was.   A broad and dark landing lay atop of it
railed off with a substantial wooden balustrade, unpainted but dark brown with age—a dim space encumbered with old boxes and ghostlike mysteries
in sheets.   I haven't the faintest idea what these
mysteries were, having never cared to investigate
them.   Behind them, almost out of sight, was a
door to a darkened room.   This also I never cared
to look into.   It was called "The Bacon-Room,"
and the name may explain why the shutters in it
were kept closed, letting in only a glimmering
light.   But though I didn't go in to examine I
knew that, somewhere in the ceiling of this room,
a trap-door gave access to the roof and the roof
beams.   This roof space was inhabited by nothing
worse than rats, I think: but it was called "The
Cock-Loft."   Of late I have realized that bacon-
room and landing must have been over the dairy
and scullery.

Near the other end of the building, tucked in at
the back between sitting-room and shop, there
was another staircase.   You got into it by a doorway in the corner of the shop, near the glass doors
there; and it led up to an end bedroom—"The
Birdy Room"—over the shop.   And this was at
any rate a less ghostlike way of going to bed than
by the scullery, though there was no carpet to make
either set of stairs feel safe and cosy.   But at

any rate no uncanny landing added terrors to these.

From one staircase to the other a passage ran against the back wall, lit by a long, low, diamond-paned window somewhere near the middle of it, over the back door. Very soft and pleasant was the light that came in that way on the old floor-boards. There was a step somewhere in the passage: it made the place all the better to scamper along, and I must have spent hours in that employ-ment. A shallow cupboard was in the wall nearly opposite the window. It held nothing more in-teresting than linen.

As the passage was at the back, so the rooms it led to were all at the front of the house, with out-look down the village street. As already ex-plained, these rooms were in a string, like those on the ground floor. First was the bacon-room over the dairy. Then, over the kitchen, a large room— huge, I thought it: the Grandmother's bedroom. Then another bedroom. Finally the "birdy room" aforesaid. Of the first of these—the bacon-room —nothing is known to me. Years afterwards I seem to have read of the Grandmother's room in "The Vicar of Wakefield"; the fact being that memories of it leapt up in my mind in apt illustra-tion of that book. Two beds stood in it, two four-posters, clothed with chintz curtains—a dainty rosebud-patterned chintz. The bed nearest the door was the one I was put into; and there I have lain, lonely and quaking, while the household seemed to have deserted me. All that could be heard was an occasional rat leaping from rafter to rafter in the cock-loft overhead.

My worst terror was particularly far-fetched. I cannot remember a time when I couldn't read at all, and I had read in some child's book—the *Child's Companion*, I fancy it was—the account of a fire, with the firebell ringing and flames licking in at the windows. And as I lay o' nights, in bed in the Grandmother's room, deserted, what more likely than that this horror should begin forthwith? I had never heard of a firebell in the village; yet I listened for the fearful clanging. I looked at the window, expectant every moment of the flames. Truly I was an absurd little ass. But there's no doubt I was frightened.

Likely enough, the very means taken to save me from fright did, in fact, excite it in me. In a recess far across the room, on a narrow table there, was burning a "twinkler," as we called it, that is to say a child's night-light. Quite safe it was, standing in a little water at the bottom of a basin; but it wasn't altogether comforting. Most of the room was gloomy in the shadow of the basin. Familiar things grew unfamiliar. A tall clothes-press near the door loomed maliciously: several pictures on the walls were as bad. Useless to remember what they were by daylight—a dark old print of George Morland's "Grey Horse," an oil-painting of a beady-eyed damsel said to be my grandmother herself as a girl—all this might be so, by daylight. But it didn't seem so at all by candlelight, or the apology for candlelight which glimmered from the twinkler. Then, the pictures grew sinister. Did not that portrait move stealthily? Was there not mischief somehow in that dark clothes-press, or hiding in the curtains of that other bed?

These terrors presumably came of loneliness. As soon as I heard the movements downstairs it seems to me I must have fallen asleep, for I have no recollection of anyone coming to me. And so I slept until broad daylight, unconscious that somebody must have gone out, early every morning, to give the keys of the stable to the carter. Every night those keys were on the dressing table tied to a long string; every morning somebody went, probably to the passage window, to let them down. Yet I never knew it until I was told years afterwards, perhaps after Aunt Susan's death, in reminiscence of her multitudinous cares in managing the indoor work of the farm.

The only other room I ever entered upstairs was that over the shop—known to children as the "birdy room." That queer name was given it, I suppose, because a striking bit of its furniture was a glass case full of stuffed birds—probably from the Amazon forests. A toucan stood in the middle of the case, large-billed, ferocious of aspect. That this collection came from the Grandmother's sailor brother is pure surmise; I never heard it stated; never heard the origin of the birds so much as mentioned. Yet their presence in that English farmhouse possibly had some romantic history; their gaudy plumage certainly gave a not inappropriate touch of colour to that room, so quiet, so homely, yet so much daintier, somehow, than the rest of the house.

Not candlelight, as in the case of the Grandmother's bedroom, but daylight—a softened reflected morning light—suffuses my memories of this "birdy room," where I used to sleep in later years. I had no night terrors there, but joyous awakings. The chintz hangings round the fourpost bed were of the same pattern as on the other beds; only, here they are remembered in cheerful morning light.

From door to window the bedroom floor slanted down considerably, suggesting, now I think of it, that there ought to have been another post under it, at the front end of the shop counter below. Still, there was no post: so, in crossing the bedroom, one went downhill to the window.

The window gave a commanding view of the Old Pollard, of Jane Charlton's tiny post-office near by, of the village street away at the back. On the right, at right angles to the window, between that and the bed, was a chest of drawers on which were various knick-knacks, though all I remember was a china cup and saucer showing fine shrimp-coloured ladies and gentlemen. To the left of the window, facing the bed and the chest of drawers, was first a roomy cupboard, and next to it a fireplace—the only bedroom fireplace in the house, I think.

It must have been a very cold Christmas afternoon, when I saw a fire actually glowing there between the curious lozenge-shaped front bars. The comfortable look of it hasn't yet died out of my memory; yet the weather must have been cold indeed to justify such an increase to the housework as a bedroom fire involves. Of this, however, I knew nothing. My occupation was to sit in the warm and gloat over the display of Christmas parcels being then, at last, brought out from their resting-place in the cupboard in readiness for the evening.

CHAPTER III

KEEPING CHRISTMAS

GREEDINESS, not so much for food as for what I was to get in the shape of presents, seems to have dulled my memory to much in those yearly gatherings at the farm which it would be pleasant to recall now if the recollections were there to be recalled, and has left remembrance chiefly of my greed. For instance, I have not forgotten how defrauded I felt to receive a present of clothes, instead of a really desirable toy, or to get a "Church Service" (its covers brass-edged, and uneven enough to jag your skin) instead of a book worth studying—a really good book about animals, or Indians, or coral islands. I remember these disillusionments: the touches of old English life that must have come so plentifully with them and would be so good to think of now have left scarcely a trace. There is an "atmosphere"—that is all. And even that may have come to me afterwards, from reading books, seeing pictures, hearing Christmas carols. Carols, in fact, were not much heard at Street Farm. None the less, the sentiment—of "Good King Wenceslas" perhaps, or of

"I saw three Ships"—seems to have pervaded the whole festivity.

Lasting over two or three days, this festivity— a yearly affair as I have said—must have meant more extra work than one cares to contemplate, to the Aunt in charge of the farm; but it may well have been a happy occasion to the Grandmother. A reunion of her family it was for her : the chief function of it being, probably, the Christmas dinner.

Twenty-one people at any rate, if not more, sat down to this meal, in the big kitchen. Sheets had been spread over the bacon flitches, to take chance contact with best coats or frocks. About half way down the room, with her back to the hearth, sat the Grandmother; her daughter Susan took the head of the table, to be handy for getting out to the copper and the cooking arrangements in the outbuildings at the back. There, at that end of the table, she carved the roast beef : while at the other end, back to window, a son-in-law carved the boiled—the "silverside," as I heard it called. Plenty of aunts and uncles and cousins filled the other places. But they were nothing to me. I was there myself —near the sitting-room door, so that was all right. It was "Christmas," and nothing else mattered. I don't even remember what there was to eat, besides the beef. I do surmise that a Christmas pudding with a sprig of holly in it was brought in

at a later stage. Yet it isn't the pudding itself I
recollect, so much as the Aunt's consternation one
year, drowned in merriment from all her guests,
at finding that pepper had been used instead of sugar
in mixing the pudding. Other food—more notice-
able though at suppertime—was mincepies, "scrap-
pies," jam-tarts. These last were made as big as
a dinner-plate, with fine crossbars of pastry atop,
showing a good thick layer of jam. "Scraps"—
very rich and tasty and indigestible—were fat slips
and slithers of the inside of pig-meat, baked crisp
and brown. When the Christmas dinner was over,
all stood up and sang the verse that begins "Praise
God from whom all blessings flow," by way of
grace.

Good-tempered religiousness was never far away.
The same company sometimes drew together in
clusters in the sitting-room at night to sing hymns.
Rather a waste of time, I always felt it, yet it didn't
matter much, more pagan delights, with presents, being sure to come on the next day, and Christmas Day
alone being frittered away with hymns. There was
no instrumental music; the untutored singing was,
almost certainly, an outrage from any artistic
standpoint, yet in the retrospect it ranks with things
as dear, as venerable, as, say, the little old churches
and the ancient carols of England. The candlelight, or lamplight rather (I wish I could remember
what the lamp looked like, or where it stood), was

yellow, soft, and steady; the hymns were good to hear—at least so far as I remember—"Hark! the Herald Angels sing," and "Oh come, All ye Faithful."

If it didn't happen to be a Sunday, something more like a "sing-song" followed; and still a sentiment of earlier times prevailed, in the peaceful mellow lamplight. A purely sentimental gush applauded the Grandmother, when she could be induced to sing songs of her own girlhood. "Before the bright sun rises over the hill," was one of these ditties, sung to the tune of "My lodging's on the cold ground." Another was "Woodland Mary" —the tune of it very warbling and suggestive of the eighteenth century.

Here too I heard a song—"Oh, Happy Tawny Moor," besides one—"We'll give to the belly, boys, ale enough," which left me wondering who the belly boys could be. But the real delight was a couple of songs contributed by an uncle (Uncle Bill the Potter). He gave us an echo of Napoleon's war—"The Local Militia Lads," which went somehow like this:

"Your wicked plots are all found out, Bonay it will not do.
  The Lo-o-cal Militia Lads will soon be after you."

"For the fifes and drums shall rattle and the bands shall
    sweetly play,
  And the Lo-o-cal Militia Lads will boldly march away."

Better still was "Bright Phœbus hath mounted his Chariot of Day." I have sometimes suspected that a priggish laughter from the younger generation may have made the singer unwilling to do more: for some of us felt "superior"—good heavens!— and may have laughed too freely, at—what? I only know I laughed, though I never really saw any joke. Somebody had taught me it was "funny" that the Uncle had translated "chariot" into "char-yot." Many subsequent years have brought proof enough that it was a sort of privilege to hear the Wessex dialect and to see a Wessex countryman—broad-faced, twinkling-eyed —enjoying Christmas by the fireside of a genuine English farm.

It came rather as a shock to me to learn—not so many years ago—that the Christmas tree was an innovation at the farm, very little older than myself. I had always thought the evening given over to that delight a real survival of the most ancient folk-life. It was the one evening of the year; a spangled candle-lit greenery that beckoned across the seasons, with messages from far-off generations. I know better now: but so it truly seemed. Besides, the Christmas presents were brought down from the "birdy room" cupboard for that evening, making it, for me, an orgy of delight. It's unlikely that I thought anything about old times in the rapture of having new things.

Christmas trees are probably all much alike— though, in my own private mind, all others I ever heard of at the time were poor trumpery things, compared to this splendour in the kitchen at the old farm. There was, however, one feature most likely singular. On the floor all round the tree stood a ring of wax candles not much bigger than a pipe-stem, pushed each into a lump of clay for a candlestick. The lumps of clay—about as big as a hen's egg—were brought of course from Uncle Bill's pottery especially for this occasion. But the use of wet clay for an impromptu candlestick was no new thing. It was, rather, a piece of real English folk-life.

On another evening—it cannot have been the same as that of the Christmas-tree party—came the Mummers. You may read about this play in Hardy's "Return of the Native," but I saw it with my own eyes—not a revival by patronizing culture, but a true survival from the Middle Ages. I need not have hidden my sight in terror on my mother's knees. Yet how was I to know? When the street door opened upon the wintry night, and oddly dressed men came shambling into our lamp-lit kitchen out of the dark, how was I to guess that this clattering intrusion must have been all arranged beforehand? or that those figures in their gay ribbon and tinsel were only quiet villagers— Bill Russell, for instance, the farm lad? Bill Russell had been sitting by the kitchen fire—at the gloomier side, to be sure—only the evening before.

And then that Mr. Ray. A joke arose about his name: for in answer to an uncle (by marriage), he called himself " Ray, sir." Had he said "Racer" or "Razor"? There was a laugh about it, and to me it seemed witty beyond words. But this was when the show was over, and those fierce strangers had ceased to be terrible and begun to talk like safe, happy countryfolk again.

I didn't see all the show, then, yet plucked up courage to see that it had to do with a feud between a Turkish Knight and King George, with a Doctor and others intervening. I saw their dread wooden-sword play on the space cleared for them before the hearth; saw King George (I expect he was "Gearge") fall down with a flump, dead; saw the Doctor come forward then and bring him to life again, with a patent application. "Some calls it 'Okum-pocum,'" the Doctor said solemnly, as he bent over the body, "Some calls it 'Okum-pocum,' some calls it 'Inkum Pinkum'; but the right name is 'Elicompayne.'"

Yet what pleased most was Little Jumping Jack, because he was so screamingly humorous. As he said his piece:

> " Here comes I, little Jumping Jack,
>   With me wife and family at my back,"

he turned round; and there, sure enough, on his back was his wife and family—a row of Dutch dolls sewn on. Was such a funny thing ever heard of?

Had it ever entered the wit of man to conceive so subtle a joke?

Wonders like these, it should be understood, were interruptions—joyous interruptions—to the prattle and games of children that were more or less continuous. For there were plenty of children—little boys and girls I have since learned to like, though I can hardly recover any impression of them from those old times. The games we had didn't often appeal to me strongly—they weren't romping enough; they were too formal, overdone with a singing ritual, too much of girls' games, in fact. What could a toddling boy do with "Tom Tiddler's Ground" or "Oranges and Lemons"? Silly stuff, I thought it. "Sheep, sheep, come home," wasn't so bad. It lent itself to real fun in scampering and wrestling.

Yet one game there was which, silly though I felt it then, suggests to me now one curious element that must have characterized all our play and prattle. We were little "countrified" children, carrying on our small doings with more or less of a dialect. The game went to the words,

"Chickamy, chickamy, Chany Trow."*

---

* "Chickamy, chickamy, Chany Trow,
  Follow me biddies wherever I go.
  Please Old Dame Blue Block,
  Tell me what it is o'clock.
  One—Come again at two;" etc.

So at least we said. But long afterwards it dawned upon me that " Chaney Trow" was probably " China Trough," and that we had really been singing a broad Hampshire dialect, hundreds of years old.

Singing it; yes, and perhaps thinking its thoughts. At any rate one thing, older than the Reformation, remains from all that else forgotten chatter. For, while I am not sure that it was then I heard nice shuddering tales about Spring-heeled Jack (though I think it must have been then), I am quite sure it was on one of those Christmas nights I heard about the strange doings in the stable and the cow-stalls. According to Corston, the carter, at midnight on Christmas Eve (or it may have been the night of Christmas Day) the horses in the stable and the cows in the stalls went down on their knees in worship of the newborn Christ.

Corston, it's true, was said to be an Irishman and a Roman Catholic. We didn't think that right. Yet still, who should know about the horses if he didn't, so fond of them as he was? So we told the legend with bated breath, renewing, in our own small persons, an emotion that may very well have been common all over England in the days of Queen Mary.

Compton's cab used to come early in the morning after the Christmas revels, to take me away, with my mother. This was soon after dawn, and we had breakfast by candlelight in the kitchen. At that dim grey hour the kitchen fire, newly built up with turfs, looked black and smoky; one had to sit pretty close to it to keep warm in the wintry air. Already, though, villagers were coming for milk served off the dresser under the window.

CHAPTER IV

SUMMER AT THE FARM

WHEN I was a small boy there were only two seasons for me; winter and summer; and whatever I saw of the back of the old farmhouse was always in the summer. The whole thing is muddled in my memory, yet the untidy blur of farmyard, pond, pasture, nettled gravel spaces, shaky palings, and so forth, is never to my fancy wanting in lustre of noon sunshine or sleepy afternoon tree shadow, of limpid morning light or long evening serenity. Whether this detail or that comes back, the air of June never fails. There are new and fragrant hay-ricks out in "the plat," a sweet-pea is in flower over the porch at the back door.

As I try to think of what I knew to be there, rather than to recover any comprehensive picture of what I actually saw, I am aware of four different regions, so to speak. On going out at the back door, a loose-gravelled yard divides the little orchard on the left from an old-fashioned and mucky farmyard on the right. And away beyond these, with a fence cutting it into two halves, or

26

"plats" as we called them, was a paddock of rough grass, rising gently to a field and a highish skyline. I will deal with these regions in the order I have given—orchard, gravelly yard, farmyard, and then plat back of all. Remember, the farmhouse is at our back now, shutting us off from the village street. We are facing southwards—towards the sunlight.

The tiny orchard, with the glass doors into the shop and the sitting-room, had only one tree that I can at all remember, and even of that I don't know whether it was cherry or pear. Sometimes a chicken-coop was on the grass under the tree, and there would be a brood of young chicks. I have seen the little yellow fluffy things, wrapped in old blanketing, taken into the sitting-room for warmth (it can't have been summer) and have watched the Grandmother pop a peppercorn, also for warmth, down each small throat. A hedge round the orchard screened it sufficiently from the street; but, even from my diminutive height, could be seen the chimneys of the Prince of Wales public-house— just where the street had narrowed down to curve ramblingly through the older and squalider part of the village. Another hedge was towards the gravel yard—a double hedge rather, screening a secluded pathway. Lilac, I am told it was; yet I can hardly believe it wasn't privet. For that word "privet" seemed one not to be used—an improper sort of word, sounding too much like the name of the building past the hedge.

Outside this second hedge the yard dog had his kennel. I was always afraid of Nep—he barked so on his chain. It was all very well for my father to walk up and caress him; my father was a grown man. For me, Nep was safer at a distance; and I gather that other children were of the same opinion. One, indeed—ignorant then that sex forbade—was promised by an uncle (it must have been Uncle Bill) Nep's first puppy, but others had not even any deceptive expectation to mollify them. They feared the dog while they admired his shaggy black and white coat. The farm seemed to have lost caste, when he was replaced by a mean-looking chocolate-coloured dog.

Somewhere near the dog-kennel there was a brick building—a bakery. You went down a step into it. Inside, on the left hand, was a long kneading-trough; a bread oven faced the door; everywhere was the comfortable scent of newly baked loaves, crisp of crust, the very thing for farm butter.

The gravelled yard is chiefly memorable for a thin crop of venomous-looking nettles growing here and there, out of the "tread," but it was in fact only a sort of open-air lobby—a wide track across to the plat or sideways to the bakehouse or to the farmyard. If there were any old barrel-

SUMMER AT THE FARM 39

hoops knocking about, they would be dumped
down here into an odd corner—that's the sort of
place the yard was. The daylight would come
back hot and dazzling from the small loose gravel
—small and loose and bleached. Pigsties and the
roughest of fencing divided it off from the farmyard. Short bits of stick lay about—the rubbishy
débris of bavins unloaded for the bread oven.
Once, being at a loss what to do there, I was
advised—and again it must have been by the
waggish Uncle Bill—to pick up every bit of stick
I could find with two ends to it. At the corner
nearest the farmyard a drinking-tub for the farm
horses stood, just below the washhouse window.
A lead gutter to the tub was run through the wall
so that water could be pumped into it from inside.

The Farmyard

The long roof of the farmhouse extended still
farther, to cover also certain outbuildings, which
shut in the farmyard from the road. Inside, just
past the water tub already mentioned, a low gate
gave access to this enclosed space. Once within
the gate you came to what was, likely enough, an
untidy scene such as would hardly be allowed now-
adays. My memory conjures up a dirty duckpond,
beyond a stretch of slate-coloured mud with a
grunting pig or two lying in it. Near at hand—
on the left—are pigsties; opposite them, on the

farther side, cowstalls and cartsheds, while from both sides the filth is trickling down into the muckheap and the pond. A glimpse of the plat out beyond—on the fourth side of the square—takes away the memory of squalor, it is so open-aired and summerlike a glimpse. Moreover, there is tolerable cleanliness and some interest quite close at hand, if you don't cross the farmyard (I think I never did) but are content to stay near those places all lying under the long roof.

Certainly it was tolerably clean along there. A causeway of stones—perhaps boulders—made a dryish pathway all along the inner wall of house and yardbuildings. The pavement was broken in one place, indeed, for when you opened the gate to go into the farmyard proper you had to step over an open drain from the sink. But that being passed, on the right-hand side were the doorways into the various buildings — the turfhouse, the stable, the barn. Only, before the barn doors were reached, came an entrance from the road outside. Big boarded gates shut out the road; but, if opened, they could let in a waggonload of corn. In the entrance, under the roof, the waggon might stand in the dry all night: it could be unloaded into the barn for threshing; for there was the threshing-floor. I could conjure up a picture of it all quite easily; yet the picture would be only conjuring. All that really stays in my memory is an impres-

sion of shadowy corners in the barn, and low
wooden partitions beside the threshing-floor—the
wood silvery-brown with age, grey with dust. The
barn, however, or rather the causeway before it,
furnishes me with an illustration to a line in
"L'Allegro": "Stoutly struts his dames before"
—yes, I know. I know what Milton must have
been thinking of. "Barn-door poultry" were
abundant on that quiet grey causeway between
farmyard and barn. Into the stable I looked, and
no more. The farm horses stood there. The turf-
house was given over to stores—big stores had to
be harvested—of fuel for the kitchen. I think it
was open from ground to roof. Ropes were hung
on the beams sometimes, to make a swing for any
child guests.

The Plats

Child play was not possible in the messy farmyard, hardly possible even in the gravelled patch
between farmyard and back door; but its home—
its summer home at least—was in those grassy
plats that lay beyond, so familiar near the house,
so beautiful farther away, leading, it seemed, to unknown fields and woods.

The fence of rough rails that cut the grassy
paddock into two began against the pigsties, shut
off the nearer side of the pond, and so stretched
into the unknown a hundred yards away. A field

gate, near the farther end, gave a way from the
first plat to the second, but it wasn't much used, at
least by me. For a tall tree—a sycamore—stood
by the fence between the gate and the pond and
I rarely wished to go farther. The tree was a thing
so graceful of growth I loved it, even then, for its
beauty; and now in my memory it stands out, as
then it stood over the grassy plat, tranquil, tall,
shapely, full-branched, shady—a sort of companion.
How many hours I must have spent in the shade of
it! Two large roots, beginning a foot or two
above the ground, had made a sort of cavern or
penthouse, in which some of us children essayed
to build a tiny house—a sort of fairy-tale house.
Our materials were only the flattest little stones
we could find, and as we had no mortar or clay, or
even dreamed such a thing would be helpful, of
course we seldom got above the second course of
stones. That didn't matter, however. The site
was obviously right; it seems to me we always
thought we were going to build a cottage there
under the tree-roots. And no failure made me
even discontented.

When things went wrong and a change was
desirable, all one had to do was to turn over on
the grass. Somewhere near at hand mallows used
to grow. So far as I know to the contrary they
were always in flower; yet it was always a glad
surprise to find the seedpods — the "bachelor's

buttons "—which could be picked out and eaten. In the shadow of the great tree, with the sunlight flickering here and there, desires grew placid enough even for a child. The hours went by unheeded, with careless prattle; the passing minutes brought all one needed.

Now and again we ventured into the farther plat, though it was too far from the farm and from one's mother to be very alluring. A granary stood in it, on mushroom-headed supports, the door of the granary being only approachable if a step-ladder was brought. I saw the inside only once or twice, but remember a golden light there, which may have been due to the corn, but was more probably the reflected light of a warm summer evening. A blue-painted winnowing-machine stood there once. It seemed to interest some grown-up people; but it didn't interest me.

Once, in this farther plat, I was inveigled into a game of cricket. Ridiculous pastime! It was only a bore to a small egotist, afraid of the ball— even of one of those white-skinned halfpenny balls from Aunt Susan's shop—and chiefly concerned to shine and be petted all the time. The sunny meadow was good, though, and the lengthening shadows.

More to my taste—something left me dissatisfied, but I can't think what—was a sort of impromptu tea brought out to a little group of us, nestling under the tarpaulin atop of an unfinished hayrick. I incline to think it was cream instead of milk with my tea produced a slight disrelish. Yet still I remember the glowing June afternoon. I remember once, too, walking in the same quarter of the plat with my mother while she counted the new ricks and seemed glad. I didn't know why it mattered.

I have said that the plats seemed to recede into the unknown—into peace and fields and woodlands. Yet I remember, very faintly, how the pottery lay on one side—very far away perhaps—a couple of hundred yards perhaps; while on the other side—the village side—a school roof could be just seen. Sounds of singing came from this building sometimes. And I resented—what? Perhaps the intrusion of the modern times upon the dreamy old world I was living in. And this is queer: the impressions of the sight and sound of the school are now all but faded from my memory. What remains strongest is summer—long tranquil shadows of trees, haymaking time, roses. The china bowls in the sitting-room window were kept full of roses.

And I think the memories are sunny because, being a puny little weak-chested chap, I was never allowed to go out into the plat to play unless the grass was dry and the weather warm—unless, in fact, the morning dews had given way to summer afternoon.

Odds and Ends

The live things on the farm have left strangely little impression on my mind: very likely I was afraid of them and avoided them. Besides the yard dog Nep there was a cat—Tiger—whose name at least seemed grand. I have spoken of two horses; but before them, contemporary with Tiger perhaps, there was one with the admired name Captain Grey. His two successors, Jolly and Lion, were respectively black and chestnut, glossy I still think, incomparably splendid I used to think. One venturesome cousin, or my brother perhaps, allowed himself to be treated to a ride on Jolly's or on Lion's back; but not me. The only ride I remember, and it's very dim, was when somebody seated me astraddle on the back of a cow. A vague feeling of summer evening and an unpeopled village lane comes back to me when I think of those two or three minutes, and makes me regret the occasion was no longer. But more to my mind was an occasional lift in an empty waggon lumbering out to the hay meadows.

Still less do I remember of the farm people, though certainly I was not afraid of them. They were too harmonious with the general atmosphere of the place to be individually conspicuous. Their voices, with the true Hampshire quality, were as much a part of the farm and its doings as the scent of new bread or of turf fires. A forceful and kindly generation of English men and women, wrestling with the problems set by England's soil and weather, had fitted themselves so ably to their provincial environment that their going out and coming in, their talk, their manners, were as "usual" as the seasons and made no more impression on me. Only when I got them apart, and out of their native habitat, did they begin to have any individuality. This, however, happened at times.

For my home was at Farnham, seven miles away along the turnpike; and my days, always happy, sometimes glowed with special radiance because the Grandmother, or an aunt or an uncle, came over to see my mother, and a feeling from the farm glorified the quiet little town. Extra things to eat no doubt contributed some of the pleasure—I might get a taste of sponge-cake then; yet it was the brilliance of the sunlight that left the enduring mark. That seems reasonable enough. With railway travelling still so inconvenient—Ash Green station, three miles from the farm, was then the best for getting to Farnham—visitors naturally only came in fair weather. Yet, on looking back to the days when they did come, I seem to see always an unusual dazzle of reflected light in the shop windows and a dancing warmth along the pavements of the little town.

The most frequent visitor was the Grandmother

— my own mother's mother — already a widow
before my memories begin. Describe her I cannot, for the reason that fancy, whenever I try, will
only conjure up pictures of one or two others since
seen—little old black-dressed farm-mistresses she
may or may not have resembled. But at any rate
she must have been of the type; so I can fancy her
at her shopping—shy, serious, yet self-possessed,
knowing herself to be a good customer, quite capable of all the business she had to do in the town
with grocer, draper, maltster, and so on. Sometimes she took me with her on these expeditions.
I remember sitting through a ceremonious occasion at a spirit merchant's, where the old lady sat
sipping a complimentary glass of wine, and the old
wine merchant was stately and very civil. Doubtless he had just receipted a bill and taken an order.

The visits of her daughter—my Aunt Susan—
were fewer—she had too many duties at home, I
think; yet for me they always had the same quality;
for they were always as a visitation from the bliss-
ful farm. But why, I wonder, does the thought
of them never come to me without thought of a
canary in a cage in a shop doorway singing so as
to be heard far along the street? That invariably
recurs. It is midday; Aunt Susan is sitting down
to sponge-cake or other light refreshment after
her journey; and through the summer air the loud
trilling of a canary comes in ringing waves—from

the boot shop, or the greengrocer's next door to it, as if the whole town was glad to have summer and Aunt Susan.

And, anyhow, I was glad; it's not very easy to see why. The visitor, it is true, was never anything but kind and good-humoured; yet she was grave, nowise austere indeed, but a little bit remote, perhaps even preoccupied. And, though I don't know, it occurs to me as possible that a special atmosphere of sisterly regard for her, of tenderness, amounting to something near veneration, may have been quickened by her during her rare visits. For though I didn't know, others knew, how the old Grandmother's comfort and the whole prosperity of the farm swung round Aunt Susan's personality. For long it had done so; from her childhood she had been untiring, self-forgetful— I didn't know it; cannot remember even very clearly what she looked like or recover any sound of her voice. I only know that her good-tempered eyes looked as if she was as truthful as she was capable and as if she had any amount of things to see to. I never heard what brought her to Farnham —it may have been licensing business connected with her shop. A few hours saw it done. Soon she went home again. That she ever slept away from the farm for so much as one night I have yet to learn.

But the most welcome visitor of all for a little

boy was William, "Uncle Bill," as we called him.
He was at that time carrying on the pottery that
had been his father's—the pottery I hardly ever
went into though it was so near the farm; and I
can guess that it was in this connection that he
came often to Farnham. Indeed, it was for him
that my father—a wheelwright in Farnham—con-
structed a pug-mill for preparing the potter's clay,
and this no doubt brought Uncle Bill to see us
several times. But my memories of him are rather
earlier than that—long before I knew that business
occupied anybody's life as a serious pursuit. Uncle
Bill—large-faced, clean-shaved, dressed in large
floppy clothes—was like a big boy himself, who
liked the same things that a little boy liked. And
in fact that was, I fancy, some of the charm of him
throughout the family. Kindly, twinkling-eyed,
tender as a child—was he not always something of
the beloved boy to his sisters? They used to tell
what a tease he was when they were all little
together; how he executed a favourite doll one of
them had, and how his sweet temper mollified them.
He used, with scissors, to cut out rows of little
paper dolls to please them; or, with clay, to twist
up tiny figures of animals—rabbits, dogs—for their
delight.

And since my own sister recalls his taking her
into the bakehouse at the farm and making for her
a dough rabbit, I can well believe that Uncle Bill

was a kindred spirit—still a happy child at heart, spite of the plentiful troubles of a man in business. Troubles he had, certainly. Once, at Farnham fair, a substantial sum of money he had received—£50, I think—was stolen from him within half an hour, and that must have been wretched news to carry back in the evening to the farm, where pounds sterling were always few. Another time he told of a visit to London, where—in the New Cut—a thief snatched a pocket-handkerchief from him, and ran off with it. Uncle Bill ran after him calling "Stop, thief!" and indignantly related to us how the callous populace had merely laughed. These incidents, however, were but the table talk of grown-up people. Quite other matters gave the guest value in the eyes of a little child.

He brought presents from London. Once, some Dutch dolls no more than an inch long, and lovely to him as to me because they were so very small. Another time there were tiny clay Japanese figures, delectable for the same reason; while yet another time my soul was delighted by a gift of "Fifty Animals in Action"—a roll of stiff paper printed with pictures of animals and stretched over two cylinders, for winding forwards and backwards. Poor fun, I think it must have been, yet how often I wound and unwound those cylinders. Great was the morning when Uncle Bill bought me a catapult. What shop he took me to I don't know; nor do I know how or why the toy soon disappeared or whether I missed it. Only, out of the haze of forgetfulness stands a roseate pink colour—the ugly puce-coloured turned handle of a catapult, and a fair though cloudy sky with trees in leaf—probably apple-trees. All the rest is gone from me.

But greatest or most surprising of all (what could not Uncle Bill manage though?) was a sight he took me to see. It was at the back of Castle Street, in one of the many yards in Farnham—probably behind the Bull and Butcher, an ancient inn now pulled down. Wherever it was, my uncle led me round a corner or two to a stable—or barn perhaps; and there, to my enraptured eyes—the door being opened—appeared an elephant, or rather the butt-end (as Mr. Kipling says) of an elephant. Was there a menagerie in the town? or a circus? I haven't the least idea. All that remains to me is so much as a little child may see, staring up at the grey and crinkled skin of an elephant's hindquarters, framed in the shadows of a dim barn. It is huge and rounded.

It was some years later, yet still in the period I am recalling—a part of my own farm memories—that Uncle Bill died. His was the first death in the family after his own father's, which was before my time. One winter morning by candlelight my mother woke me to say that she was going away for the day—Compton's cab had come to fetch her in a hurry, because "Uncle Bill was very ill." Late at night she came back. Uncle Bill was dead.

Then I heard how, years earlier, he had fallen from a hay waggon on to his head, and this was supposed to be the cause of his breaking down so suddenly. More likely it was a stroke of paralysis that laid him low. At any rate he lay unconscious all day and died in the evening. The pottery had to be given up then. The buildings were razed to the ground; the site was absorbed in Farnborough Park. I couldn't make out where it had been, when last I passed, some years ago.

Of the younger brother John, my venerated friend in his old age, my memory is a blank as to this earlier period. He was probably away at work on the farm during most of my waking hours. Likewise the other three sisters do not come into any picture of the farmhouse life. My own mother Ellen had come away to Farnham at her marriage: the youngest, Mary, was married and in London. Between these two in years, Ann, unmarried, after many changes came to live and to die in my house. From her (as from John) I came to learn many details of the family. In spirit she was indeed, as they all were, bound up in an affectionate family piety. Yet into my direct knowledge she didn't come at that time. Susan, William, and their mother are all I can remember.

But the glamour of the whole household never

deserted me for long. Up and down the streets of the old town a few elderly men were known to me as men having some acquaintance with Farnborough in those days—old Seymour, who sold fowls or ducks from a basket, possibly having walked the seven miles to the farm to get them; old Natt Attfield—strange, straddling, much-afflicted man, notable for having got up again after the knell had been rung for him, and living many years afterwards; and especially Mr. Avenell. He had been a postboy in the days before railways, his headquarters being at Farnborough. Sometimes, too, messengers, or acquaintances, came to wait on my mother, with gossip or with parcels from her old home. Amongst the latter I recall especially a Mr. Goodfellow. I have never, before or since, seen so large and shiny a bald head as his. A messenger—Tom or Jim Watts, once a carter at the farm—had also a memorable head, not because it was bald—it was grey and shaggy—but because of its immense size. I remember looking at his hat—a tall beaver—he had placed, on its crown, in a corner of the room and wondering at its proportions. I thought it would hold a bushel.

What Jim Watts had come for is more than I can say. He always offended my mother by addressing her familiarly by her Christian name as if she were still a little girl at the farm. Presumably he never came without some parcel of produce—

one of Aunt Susan's loaves perhaps, or some home-made buns, or a "lardy" cake. Or perhaps it was pig-killing time at the farm, and he brought a treat of "scraps," or souse, or hogs-puddings. Once, by some such conveyer, we had chitterlings— "chidlins," as they were called—and that is the only time I ever tasted that so succulent dainty. Though I was ill afterwards, I have always held that the chitterlings were worth it. And anyhow it is worth while to have set eyes on Jim Watts.

Shadow of a dream though he has become to me, still it is part of a dream of old English rural life. Thinking of Jim Watts (ah, how drunk he used to get sometimes!) or of the farmhouse economy he belonged to, I feel that I have looked upon England not only in recent eras but in long past ones; and so a sense of great continuity spreads over me.

PART II

CHAPTER V

THE POTSHOP

WILLIAM SMITH, potter and farmer, was born at Cove in 1790. When the boy was quite little his father died, leaving a widow with several small children, and William, the eldest—after three days' schooling—had to go to work. One tale about him in these early years is preserved. Smallpox was raging: to escape inoculation the boy "got under the table." There was "an image of Bonaparte" on the table; and when at last little William was dragged out he upset the table and all. He lived to laugh long afterwards that he had "smashed Bony-party."

It was by Frimley parish that work was found for him: he was apprenticed to a potter. Of course he was too young, "but then, he delighted in it so." And, delighting in it, he made himself master of his trade. At nineteen years old he bought the pottery business at Farnborough, the stock-in-trade being valued at £19. Mr. Callaway, the owner of the premises, objected at first. "It's

too much, my boy," he said, "you shan't have it."
Yet it was this same Mr. Callaway who afterwards
arranged the matter, perhaps on easy terms.

The district was pretty thick with potteries at
that time, there being as many as thirteen thriving
kilns in the village of Cove alone, to say nothing
of the adjoining villages Farnborough and Frimley.
The ware was then of the simple red kind, well
glazed; but a thinner biscuit-coloured ware was
found when the "bank" at Farnborough was at
last levelled; and, as further token that the craft
had long been widely practised in that neighbourhood, excavations (notably when the Alma was
built) have shown the soil to be full of potsherds,
often little bits ("shords") no bigger and no thicker
than a halfpenny.

What was the attraction? Of clay there was no
great quantity. True, at Cove Common a few
"pockets" of clay were a temptation to "squatters";
but in the main the clay had to be brought from
Tongham or even from Farnham Old Park, eight
miles away. There was a "clay-audit" on April 1,
when the potters journeyed to Farnham Castle to
pay their year's account to the lord of the manor—
the Bishop of Winchester. For a time the Barrett
family rented the land at Old Park, and then the
audit was held at the Barretts' house in Bridge
Square at Farnham.

It is likely that the plenty of fuel on the common

was what drew so many potteries to the neighbour-hood. No coal came into the district excepting by the canal, for there was no railway. There was a little peat at Cove Common, "where the camp is now" (1905). A rough fuel called "tods"—a sort of earth that will burn—cut rather larger than turfs, could be had. But turfs were the mainstay, those from Frimley Common being especially good.

More will have to be said on this by and by. It is enough now that William Smith may be thought of, at nineteen years old, as having a trade at his fingers' ends, besides the premises, with some of the material, for carrying it on. Yet how much else he needed! His three days of schooling had not taught him to read and write, still less to keep accounts. The clay and the fuel had to be brought to the pottery, the finished product to be sent away. Lastly, customers themselves had to be found; for no goodwill had been bought with the stock-in-trade. All these difficulties the young man had to face, alone perhaps. Or perhaps not alone. When he married his first wife I never heard, nor yet when she died. She didn't live long, yet long enough, it may be, to see him overcome the last-mentioned difficulty, about customers.

The plan he adopted sounds simple: he took samples to London of the ware he could supply, and booked orders accordingly. I mean, "obtained" orders, which he carried in his head, since his want of schooling had left him unable to use books at all. But simple though this sounds, not to say primitive, it must in fact have been a difficult job, requiring a certain sort of courage, because of its very primitiveness. Grant that the stock-in-trade probably contained the tools and the clay for potting the ware, the prepared lead for glazing it, the turf for burning it in the kiln; it is yet hard to understand how a frugal and cautious man could either care to spend a whole kiln of firing and a month's time on making a few samples, or how he would dare to risk more. Either course was hazardous—a gamble, of a sort not enjoyed in William Smith's family. But that was not all. Even to-day it would be tiresome to convey samples of earthenware into and through London; but at that time there was no train, no motor-car or taxi-cab, to set William down where he wanted to go and to bring him home again at night. He had to travel to London by coach, to traverse the streets on his feet, to sleep in London at night. And it was all strange to him. To the best of my belief he had never been in London before—never farther than he might walk along the turnpike, across the lonely heaths.

True, the journey, though strange to him person-ally, was by no means unprecedented in his trade. Many, if not all, of the local potters had some connection in London; moreover there was one inn at Westminster they used to stay at, where William Smith also was introduced, with consequences momentous to him, for he married his second wife from there. But that was long afterwards. It did nothing to diminish the adventurousness of his first visit to London.

The venture prospered. The young man got orders and went back to his work at the Farnborough kiln. The premises included a row of three or four cottages; and to one of these he now brought his mother from Cove, with his brothers and sisters. The brothers went to work in the potshop. Presumably William himself, with his wife, had another of the cottages; and certainly he was left a widower before the next ten years were out. But in all this time his business was increasing and his journeys had to be periodically made to London.

CHAPTER VI

THE SECOND MARRIAGE

THE following entry stands on the flyleaf of
William Smith's family Bible:

> John Blackburn
> Came Up to London
> on Thirsday the
> 23 of June 1785
> and I got in
> on Setterday the
> 25 day

The rough piece of notepaper on which the above
is written has been stuck into the Bible with more
modern stamp-edging. On the other side, partly
scratched out as if it were a false start, is written:

> John ~~Blackburn June 2~~
> ~~day~~ 1785 23
> June
> ~~Jim~~ and I got ~~Hither~~
> the 2— and I Stopt at
> Wetherby all Night
> and the Next N——
> at Doncaster and I got
> to lon

I never heard why this John Blackburn left Yorkshire or how much of his journey he did afoot.
He had five shillings in his pocket and conceivably

JOHN BLACKBURN

he made friends with various drivers, for he carried a handful of whips with him, being a whipmaker by trade. The place where he "got in" on that "Setterday" in the midsummer of 1785 was an inn somewhere in Westminster—the Brewer's Arms in Millbank Street, near the river and the barges. He took service there as potboy; but eventually he married the innkeeper's daughter and became himself landlord of the inn. Now this was where the potters used to put up from Farnborough and Cove; and so John Blackburn and his wife got acquainted with William Smith, and it was their daughter Susannah who became in time Susannah Smith.

There is a picture—a little old coloured drawing, about seven inches by nine—of John Blackburn in his glory; at least it is credibly said to be he, though I can hardly believe that he ever, in the flesh, looked such a fool. He had his faults; but imbecility was not one of them. The artist, however, was no physiognomist; and it seems to have sufficed John Blackburn to be shown dressed in long snuff-coloured coat and silver-buckled shoes, the owner of a beer cellar and beer barrel. Lest there should be any doubt as to the buckles, the silver is put in in spelter; or even, it may be, in real silver.

There is a companion picture of John Blackburn's wife—a less dingy picture than her husband's. The lady is shown, if stupid of face (did the artist draw faces by rule?), stately of deportment. Instead of a dull cellar, a cheerful shop makes her background. Plenty of china is about, with a colour familiar to my eyes. On the floor is a surprisingly long cradle, empty; the baby to fit it sits, prim, on the lady's lap.

Who was the baby? Can it have been Susannah herself, my own grandmother? I have never been able to ascertain. Susannah had a sister, Lydia, and a brother, Tom; and there may have been others. Anyhow, there is the mother, of whom I never heard a word, but of whom I am disposed to think highly, partly because of this picture. For she must have taken some wholesome pride in herself and her belongings, or such an ass of a painter would never have thought of getting those pleasant details together. I hesitate to say that his more natural place was in the beer cellar, with the old landlord. He may have been quite a good fellow, albeit a poor artist. All unawares he got much of the eighteenth century into these two drawings, and especially the gossipy tea-drinking side of it is shown forcibly in the portrait of Mrs. Blackburn.

Other things besides this picture—notably the character and ways of her daughter—lead up to a belief that the mother was a kindly and sensible woman, an excellent housewife too. She probably

MRS. BLACKBURN

—

died soon—one hears of John Blackburn presently
having a housekeeper; but the daughter Susannah
at least was well educated, as education went then
—she went to a boarding-school—and was indubit-
ably of devout and some religious outlook. I
always suppose she got this from her mother, and
I have sometimes thought there must have been
some of the sincere spirit of John Wesley in that
house, although Westminster Abbey near by gave
it a strong Church of England bias.

None of these things can be ascertained now.
Nothing definite is known for ten years, and then,
on January 6, 1821, William Smith, widower, of
Farnborough, was married to Susannah Blackburn,
at the Church of St. John the Evangelist, Westminster.

They must have had tremendous confidence in
one another, these two; or they must have been
very much in love. At any rate, from the wife's
point of view, the circumstances were not exactly
ideal.

Whether she had ever been out of London before
I do not know; she had never seen her husband's
home, or his people. It was a venture in the dark
for her, almost literally; and there is reason to
believe that the country darkness made an impression on her she never lost. Years afterwards it
was told of her that she disliked the country lanes
at night and longed for street lamps.

Returning to Farnborough by coach, presumably on the same day as their wedding, the pair would be entering the desolate heath country not long before the early dusk of that winter afternoon, and the last miles must have been traversed after nightfall. Perhaps the moon was up: I have never heard; but the heath must have been solitary in the extreme.

Alighting from the coach at the Ship, where the by-lane to Farnborough branches off from the turnpike, they had tea (?) at that inn, where Mrs. Wise the landlady received the young wife with a kindness that was never forgotten; and so, from the Ship, they walked home, in the winter night, about a mile to the cottage at the pottery. I should like to think that William Smith's mother, from the cottage two or three doors away, made herself truly pleasant, but it's by no means sure that she would. Be that as it may, Susannah may well have gladdened to enter a warm, candle-lit cottage, and to hear voices again, after the miles of dark and silent heath. The solitudes strike one's fancy: William was of course enough to make up for them; otherwise it must have been a dreadful change for the girl—from a busy London inn to this lonely hamlet, from thronged streets to dark country lanes where, at night, the stillness grows almost painful to listening ears.

CHAPTER VII

THE POTTER TURNS FARMER

HAVING married the daughter of a fairly well-to-do man, William Smith began to be of more importance in his parish. Moreover, sundry business conveniences became possible that had been out of his reach before.

One inconvenience had been that of carriage. It was one thing to get customers for his ware: to get the goods delivered to them was another. The Basingstoke Canal had to be used, though it was a mile or two from the pottery and involved cartage and precious time at the home end, and must have cost further cartage and time in London. There was no help for it, but packing the ware on the barges was a business in itself—a business so arduous that its details left an indelible mark on the potter's mind. What it had meant to him his family—unborn as yet —realized years afterwards, when, on his death-bed, his wandering wits harked back and he was heard giving orders as he packed an imaginary barge. "Come on! Let's have 'em along!" he would shout impatiently, as if at laggard labourers. During ten days of illness many hours were troubled in such a way. The crazy speech was so vivid that the watchers could almost see their father as a young man, sweating and toiling to get another load of pottery stowed properly on a barge for London.

But as a reality, outside the man's fretted brain, this trouble came to an end soon after the second marriage. Borrowing the wherewithal from his father-in-law, the potter got a team of his own, that made him independent of barges and hire-carts and enabled him to send by road the whole way; for a team and waggons were a part of Street Farm, which he now took over.

Nothing, indeed, could have been handier than to have this farm. Its fields surrounded the pottery: the farmhouse and outbuildings were scarce a furlong away. If there was a drawback it was that the house was too large. But, to an energetic housewife, this was hardly an inconvenience—I never heard any suggestion of the sort. And so far as I know the ground was in good order. The previous tenant, a nurseryman, had at least not neglected manure. A huge heap was so over-valued in the stock-in-trade that the price of it was always afterwards spoken of as a heavy burden for a long time round the inexperienced farmer's neck. The farm did not belong to the same landlord as the pottery: it was a part of the Farnborough Park estate.

So William Smith took the farm, borrowing £400 from his father-in-law for starting in business. At the same time old John Blackburn advanced a similar sum to his own son Tom, one of the conditions being that the two should take care of their sister Lydia Blackburn, an imbecile. But there was one thing the farmer would not do, though Tom Blackburn (a sailor) seems to have tried to work it. Nothing would prevail on William Smith to receive Lydia as an inmate of his house.

His house, not his cottage at the potshop. He left the cottage and took up his dwelling at Street Farm. And since that was larger than was needed, while the young wife was nowise afraid of work, lodgers were taken. The rooms let were those two at the far end of the building, connected by a staircase, namely the room on the ground floor which afterwards became a grocery shop, and the bedroom over it—the "birdy room" of my own recollection. Mr. Morant's steward and the steward's wife (Mr. Morant afterwards became lord of the manor and owner of Farnborough Park) were the first tenants. A child—daughter of these two (Oliver was their name)—was a great nuisance to Mr. Smith.

But eventually a less desirable tenant came, in the person of old John Blackburn himself. The farm had been taken in his name; he had advanced the money for buying the stock; he could not have been refused even if his son-in-law had been so minded. And perhaps the son-in-law was not so minded at first, for who could be a better lodger, or more acceptable to his wife, than her own father?

But the arrangement proved to have drawbacks. Old Blackburn brought with him his housekeeper (disrespectfully spoken of in later days as "Old Mother Wilson," "an ill-tempered old woman"), and two extra rooms were wanted—the middle sitting-room and what was afterwards the bacon-room, next to the "birdy room"; whereby the farmer, with his now increasing family, had only two bedrooms at his own disposal, besides the kitchen for a living-room downstairs.

The mere presence of these two people in the house was enough to give an unfavourable impression, without their possessing really the disagreeable character afterwards attached to them. If they were the cause of occasional family jars, that sufficed; the farm children were sure to lay on them all the blame of their father's irritation. But it must be owned he seems to have had some provocation. His son John said many years later, of Blackburn, "he was a tyrannical old fellow," and, not content with holding the reins (the farm being held in his name), he "wanted to shake 'em. And that wouldn't do at all." This was corroborated by John's elder sister, Ann, according to whom Blackburn was a cruel, not a good man. Her own gentle and considerate spirit was indeed shocked. Blackburn, she said, used to twit her father upon the money lent—an exasperating thing to a man of spirit, who could not afford to retort.

And even his play was exasperating—done to tease, perhaps. Certainly the farmer-potter was teased and disquieted (being of prudent and timid disposition in some things) since old Blackburn loved to play tricks with the little children—such as swinging them round by the arms, or carrying them on his shoulder and pretending to let them slip.

Such things may not have been meant unkindly; but they were not endearing. It's not surprising that no kind word was afterwards spoken of the perpetrator of them; and I have a strong suspicion that his death was felt as a considerable relief at last. I have no date for it; no particulars of it, save a pair of odd memories—the farmer's daughter Ann's again. She was old and grey-haired herself when she recalled how, being but a little girl, and standing at the gate by the village street, she heard a neighbour say, " Grandfather's dead, then?" and how an elder sister—my own mother—asked her, " Did you hear grandfather groaning?"

CHAPTER VIII

THE POTTERY

I.—*Manufacture*

ALTHOUGH William Smith took to farming willingly, he was quite inexperienced at it, whereas at pottery he was a skilled workman, and that remained his central business to the end. Of the use the farm was to him much will have to be said; but for a little while we must give further consideration to the potting.

And first of the clay. How it had to be fetched from Farnham has been told. Here, of course, the farm waggon came in handy at once. John Smith, the potter's second son, told me that he himself had been to the Old Park claypits with the waggon.

Until the pug-mill already mentioned was introduced the clay, being brought home, was put into pits (two pits) in layers, with shovelfuls of sand. Then it was well watered, and so remained twenty-four hours. From the pits it was taken out in rolls and spread on the floor in one of the potshop "houses." There men, barefoot, trod it "into little ruts," picking out any stones their feet found.

It's odd: the names of three stools used in the potting have come down to me, and some account

THE POT-SHOP

of the work with them. One stool was called "Broad-ass." Sometimes the potter himself, not finding this stool in his workshop, would sing out, "Bring me Broad-ass." Another stool went by the name of "Old Cockety." But perhaps the most useful of the three, and not the least quaintly named, was a one-legged stool known as "Nobody."

"Nobody" was invented, or introduced at the Farnborough pottery, by one Ninety Harris—no connection, so far as I know, with the well-known Harrises of Wrecclesham Potteries, but himself a skilled workman and the son of a skilled workman.

It was when the workshops were being extended (presumably there had been an increase of trade) that Ninety, a young man then, found an odd end of plank lying about and got a carpenter to bore a hole in the middle of it and put in a leg. This was the origin of "Nobody." Ninety Harris used it to sit upon, while he was making the final preparation of clay before rolling it up into lumps to "throw" on to the wheel. He sat at a bench, working the clay up into a paste under the heel of his hand. It had already been trodden, but now the tinier pellets of dryness had to be worked out—for in a pot or pan they would have burst in the burning. So the potter sat picking them out, throwing them into the "squibber" by his side, swaying to and fro, with a pushing motion, "exactly like making up butter," and putting the lumps of clay aside in a heap for carrying to the wheel. Working so, he needed no fixed seat, but this one-legged "Nobody" swayed to his movements, giving him all the support he wanted. No one in the shop had seen such a thing before; but all were glad to use it after Ninety Harris had shown the way. When not in use, "Nobody" lay on its side on the floor.

At the wheel, a potter sat on a "horse"—a wooden trestle with a cushion; but sometimes a short man could not reach to make a large pan without standing on the horse, though I cannot think how he worked the treadle in that case. His first care was to "throw" the prepared lump of clay on to the middle of the wheel; and the larger lumps, "as much as a man could lift," took some throwing. Next, moistening it with water from the squibber, the potter "trued" the clay with his hand to the centre of the wheel; and then got his thumb into it—or his hand, and finally his arm for the larger things—to "pull it up." This was no easy job for a short man.

The squibber was a tub of water which stood by the potter's side and gradually got full of clay. A sponge was kept in it, or near it. Of tools, apart from apparatus, there were very few. One, however, there was: the "ribber"—a thing made of yew, with a foot allowing it to be set against the base of the pot; and so it was held to the sides, to give them a grooving. A potter usually made his own ribbers and kept them carefully washed. Moreover, if he went to another shop he did not leave them behind for any successor, but was jealous to take them with him. Something more elaborate was occasionally used, to give a moulding to the pot. A certain Mrs. Clayton (of whom more is to be told) was very clever at cutting out these moulds.

After the ware had been potted, and before it could be put into the kiln for burning, it had to be dried. Fires of turf (or, according to a later account, cordwood, preferably of oak) were kindled in the open sheds: round the walls the raw pots were stacked in rows about waist high, with the fires under them. There was no chimney. Smoke poured out from the sheds, and sometimes, drifting across a neighbouring landowner's park, was a great nuisance to him.

At this stage lead, for glazing, was put on. The "pigs" of lead, brought from London two tons at a time in the waggon (here again the farm was usefully co-operative), were stored in the old mother's cottage, Dame Smith's at the end of the row. Two and a half hundredweight each they weighed, and needed preparation themselves, as the clay had done.

A curious and lengthy process, was this "crushing," as they called it. A furnace, divided into two compartments, held fire on one side and the lead on the other. A rake, hung on a swivel (but I do not understand how) communicated somehow with the lead; and as soon as the lead began to "flow" the man in charge had to begin raking it backwards and forwards, and continue until all was liquid. Then the raking had still to go on as the lead cooled, to bring it to a fine powder, but the powder was not cold enough to be handled for several days. A fine wire sieve at last separated from the powder any lump that had escaped; and then the glazing of the pots could begin.

This was the most injurious part of all the work. The pots, dried sufficiently for handling, were moistened so that the lead-dust would cling to them; and although, in later years, the dust was put on with a brush, for very long it was sprinkled on by the workman's own fingers. A time came at Farnborough pottery when this was commonly done by a man spoken of as "Old Jack"; but this was not until the master potter himself had permanently crippled his own hands at it.

"Setting the kiln"—arranging the ware in it for burning—was ticklish work, which William Smith could entrust to no one but himself, until years afterwards, when his son William (the Uncle Bill of my own memories) was man enough for it. By about two in the afternoon the pots, " set " in the morning and slightly hardened by a light fire, were fit to bear the weight of the morning's " setting." This lasted three days, by which time the potter, usually clean in his dress, was "as black as a sweep," and the kiln was ready for burning. Sprays or bavins were the favourite fuel. A gauge showed when the pots had sunk sufficiently; and after three more days the fires were raked out and the kiln could be left to cool. It took a week, so that from first setting to final emptying a fortnight had gone by. There were then four to five waggonloads of new ware ready for delivery.

As for the delivery—when the farm waggon replaced the canal barge, delivery was still such a business as to make me wonder how it could ever have been carried out at all by the earlier method. But before all that can be described there is a tale about the kiln to be told, illustrative, as it seems to me, of a phase now quite gone from the English countryside.

I have no date for it; but from the vivid recollections the potter's children had of the episode I infer that it happened after their Grandfather Blackburn was dead and gone, and when they were old enough to be impressed by a sense of mysterious trouble hanging over their father. They knew that his pottery business was affected and that he was himself in jeopardy.

For there came a period when the kilns of ware began to go wrong in burning. Did they sink? No. The potter's son (my own uncle) did not remember that his father ever had a kiln sink. "You see," he said, "there is the right way to stack it with pots, and to fire it, and——" and, in short, the old potter always did it right. The series of disasters, which all but ruined him, could not be traced to any negligence in that way.

There had been an ash-tree growing up beside the kiln and overhanging it. The tree and the kiln had figured in more than one painting in the Royal Academy, people admiring their picturesqueness. However, the tree had died and the potter had had it cut down, leaving the top of the stamm level with the top of the kiln. A huge stamm it was, for an ash-tree—three feet over or more. Not only was he proud of it; he used it as a bench to put the ware on, as he emptied the kiln—from the top, of course.

One day a horrifying thing was detected. Every piece of ware, as it came out, was found to be utterly worthless. Shapely, well baked, and with the glaze all as it should be, it yet contained innumerable bubbles and tiny aircracks, as fine as a hair. So one kiln was spoilt. It represented about three weeks' output.

And so too, without intermission, kiln after kiln went wrong, until there had been six or perhaps

seven failures in succession. The potter nearly
went out of his mind. My uncle—a little boy then
—remembered seeing him, standing up to receive
the ware from the top of the kiln, and, as each
piece was handed to him, throwing it crashing to
the ground, whence the heaps of sherd were taken
away by the cartload. He was indeed all but
ruined. At night, with fear of a debtors' prison
before him, he wandered about his bedroom,
muttering, "I shall go to Winchester Gaol."

One evening—it was a Saturday—a tailor came
along. A little Irishman he was, a kindly man who
had travelled a good deal. And the potter would
not order the suit of clothes he needed, because he
could not pay for them. But he told his troubles
to the tailor, who listened sympathetically and
asked, "Are there any rats about the kiln?" For
he had known of similar disasters, caused by rats
penetrating the floor of the kiln, and so letting air
in. That was an idea: in this case, however, there
were no rats. So the tailor left without his order.

The next day (Sunday) the despairing man
wandered to the scene of his troubles. And he sat
down, with his back against the bank and his feet
against the stamm of the ash-tree. And presently
the stamm gave way before him, crumbled, and
rolled in little pieces to the foot of the bank. And
with that the mystery of months was solved.

For it proved to be that the dead roots under the

kiln had been "perished" by the great heat, and, as effectually as rat-holes, had "aıred" the kiln from outside while the ware was still glowing hot. That was all. But it had wellnigh broken the potter. Just in time the discovery saved him. He had the kiln rebuilt, and the next batch of ware was all right.

CHAPTER IX

THE POTTERY

II.—Delivery

It is hard to think how the ware had ever been got to its destination by canal barge. Sending it to London by road, even with the farm to furnish waggon and horses, was business enough. Those children of the farm, whom I was to recognize afterwards as my uncle and aunt, remembered it with something like enthusiasm, and were never weary of describing it, even when they were themselves old and tottering and grey. Twice a week for three weeks the waggon went and came back; after that it waited a week or so while another burning yielded another five or six loads; and then the journeying began again. This must have gone on for years; yet the interest in it never seems to have grown stale. And certainly it touched many sides of the life that was England's at that time.

First came the duty of loading the ware into the waggon—a tricky business, not so prolonged as the loading of a barge had been, yet every bit as difficult. The potter always did this himself, permitting help only from his own son or from one trusted man named Siggery. From the way it was spoken of I got the impression that the loading involved almost a mystery to be jealously guarded; but I may have been mistaken. In any case, besides the ordinary precautions, the ordinary care anyone may imagine, to prevent breakages and to put up a load neither too heavy nor too light for the horses—besides this there were other points to be considered.

Seeing that the waggoner—Jim Watts his name was—couldn't read names but only numbers, while there were various places for him to go to, the load had to be put up, and marked too, so that he could make no blunder, but take the pieces out in their right order. Straw separated the different consignments, which also had chalk marks, agreeing with the invoices. Another point was to get the load packed so that it could be properly counted and invoiced. Here the potter's own want of schooling had been a serious difficulty, before his second wife could manage the invoicing. Still, as unlettered men will, he had mastered this obstacle for himself. He had mastered it so effectively that no others could match him at counting up a waggonload of pots. His son used to speak of his quickness with wonder. A good exercise in mental arithmetic he esteemed it, at which his father was "sharp as a needle."

Still, no doubt invoices were an improvement,

and the potter's London wife, with her boarding-
school education, made them out, putting the
"casts" in their proper columns, with admired
neatness. And so, the ware having been piled up
about two feet higher than the raves—the edge-
rails—of the waggon and secured with withes (that
was before the days of plentiful and cheap ropes),
a start could be made, when proper arrangements
had been also made for Jim Watts and the farm
boy with him. For this purpose (and it was only
needful in bad weather) a shallow coop or tilt, just
high enough to keep the man and boy dry, was
formed by bending withes over the head of the
waggon and covering them over with sacks or a
tarpaulin. It was suggested to me, but without
much conviction, that a sack slung under the
waggon provided a sort of hammock for the boy.

At two o'clock or soon after on Monday morning Jim Watts started, with his long team of three
horses in a row—four horses, I was once told, but
the smaller number is the likelier. Past the wide
heaths, by way of Bagshot and Egham or of
Chertsey, he made for Hounslow, where he came
by three or four o'clock in the afternoon and
stopped the night. Next day he started soon
enough to deliver his load in London—the Borough
and Whitechapel usually—and get out again before
the team would find the streets too busy; and so
his homeward journey was but a reversal of the

other. He put up at Hounslow again on the Tuesday night; on Wednesday afternoon he was due back at the pottery, so as to be ready to start for a second journey to last from Thursday to Saturday.

It sounds simple enough, yet the expedition must have been tolerably full of detail in fact, requiring some arrangement. The boy, being an inmate of the farm, had to be furnished with food A flag basket was given him, holding a lump of bacon and a half-gallon loaf. The waggoner himself needed money on the journey. Who paid for his food and lodging I don't know: but at any rate the master had to provide him for tolls on the turn-pike. Threepence for each horse was the charge: a receipt was given which franked a driver through at least one or two 'pikes farther. Even so the tolls for the up journey came to as much as twelve or fourteen shillings.

This was for the up journey, however. Often the return was managed free, by bringing a load of manure; for, with a view to the improvement of the land, landowners had got manure exempted from tolls. Hence trotters, rags, and other refuse, made a frequent load in the potter's waggon, to his advantage as a farmer. But many other sorts of things were brought. Lead has been men-tioned as an .occasional load. Sometimes there was old furniture, which the connoisseur gentry did not care to trust to less careful conveyance; and now and then, so laden, the waggon had to travel on, even as far as to Winchester. For the reason already given—namely, the need of a trustworthy conveyance, not always available—one load of furniture had to lie in London for three months, before an opportunity occurred to get it home. Amongst others who made this use of the waggon was "Squire Timm" from Somerset House, who rented Farnborough Grange for a time.

Meanwhile, imagine the potter-farmer at home, busy indeed at getting ready for another kiln, yet anxious for his ware and his valuable team on the road, and growing more anxious as the hour for return drew near. It's said that, by laying an ear to the ground, a listener could hear the returning waggon as far off as Frimley Grove—two miles perhaps, as the crow flies. This indeed indicates a countryside and a highroad lonelier than can be easily imagined in these days of motor-traction; at that quiet era, however, horseowners could recognize their own horses' hoof-beats a long way away, and William Smith was not likely to listen less keenly than many others. He had some provocations too to be anxious. Jim Watts, so trustworthy in other respects, was unwise, to say the least, in his enjoyment of beer. (Many years afterwards I saw him myself, very red-faced and jolly, driving a little van through Farnham Street in the Farnborough direction. Such a look, on a driver's face to-day, would certainly draw the attention of the police to him.) So it was sometimes as late as half-past four before the waggon got back on Wednesday or on Saturday. At such times the master could not contain himself for anxiety. "I've known him," one of his daughters said, "set off to meet the waggon; and get as far as the Ship, perhaps," away on the turnpike.

CHAPTER X

THE WARE, CUSTOMERS, ETC.

USUALLY the pottery-ware was reckoned in "casts" made up in so many pieces—12, 14, 32, 48, and so on, according to their size; a big pan, made of clay as much as a man could lift on to his wheel, being equal to 64 of the smallest size. The wholesale price of a cast was half a crown, delivered. The commonest pots were pipkins, ranging from the size of teacups to basins for two or three gallons. They were useful for cooking. If the potter had turnip-greens—a favourite food—left over from dinner, he would urge his wife to "get a new pipkin" to warm them up in. Other common ware was paintpots, and also "benisons" or "venisons" —I never could be quite sure of the word. I heard it, once, in an enumeration of the different products of the pottery: "bedpans for London hospitals; stoolpans" ("nasty things they were") "for children's chairs; and then there was nests of benisons . . ." but at this point the catalogue was cut short by my asking what benisons were. They were bowls made to fit into another so as to be, when all together, a solid mass of ware, and in capacity ranging from a pint to a peck. Of their uses a little more may be said by and by.

One other product there was which recalls Ninety Harris again, or rather Ninety's father, John Harris. He it was who made those moneypots of which I once owned one. Like a squat pineapple it was, on a squat stem and stand, and it stood about seven inches high in all. Harris used to pick out "marbly" clay, whatever that may be, for a moneypot. The little leaves were stuck on in rows all round. Smooth and glazed and nicely burned, the thing had something of the reddish-yellow colour of a pineapple; and at the top the point was divided by a slot big enough to admit a penny; indeed, it was slightly bigger, for, unless the pot was smashed, the only way to get out a penny that had once been put in was to place a dinner-knife inside the slot, holding the moneypot upside down and shaking it until the penny came slithering out—but that was joy—on the blade of the knife. John Harris was gifted also at pinching out, in clay, the figures of dogs—greyhounds and so on; but these I never saw.

Besides hospitals, Whitechapel Prison was supplied. Once, in all innocence, the waggon came away with a prisoner hidden in the straw packing of the pots that had been delivered. After that it was not permitted to bring the packing away. The straw had to be sacrificed and the

WARE FROM THE POTTERY

waggon came away empty. It was, in fact, a tiresome affair, this escape : the potter had a deal of trouble from it.

Seasonal trades made a difference. "The painting season," for instance, was mentioned to me once as affecting the pottery; and I surmise that in the spring, house decorators bought lots of new paintpots. More certainly the pottery was concerned in Jewish celebrations. The potter's son John (he was often facetious and twinkling-eyed when an old man) remarked, "I used to know a lot more about religion than I do now. There was a lot of Jews in Whitechapel at that time, and all their feast-days I used to know as well as anything." Any vessel—pan or pipkin—used at the Passover was destroyed, to the great satisfaction of the potters of Cove and Farnborough. And one of the shops William Smith supplied in Whitechapel did an exceptionally large business with Jews.

Of course all this involved the potter himself in periodic journeys to London to see customers. He travelled by coach to call on "the Shorters," "the Schramms," "the Phillipses"; and it was related—not without a laugh—"how cross he used to come home, because the Phillipses had been 'snorky' to him." They had excuses. Now and then it had not suited the potter to execute an order exactly. Either for convenience of loading in the waggon or of burning in the kiln, pots had been sent of different cast from those ordered. But the Phillipses—confound them!—had a copying-press, and were able to prove the potter in the wrong. And, being "big people," they were "snorky," as he used to say.

A more excusable annoyance arose in another way. Although the London connection was well established, the potter found it needful to keep on good terms not only with the principals but with the head-clerks too of the firms he supplied. These gentlemen expected to be remembered at Christmas; and very cross it used to make Mr. Smith, because they hardly scrupled to give him a reminder of what they looked for, as the season drew near. Geese, reared on the farm—ah, that blessed farm!—sufficed; but the touch of blackmail in the practice was none the less annoying.

Yet the journeys to London were by no means all annoying. A coach ride in itself cannot well have been other than interesting and must have been often delightful to a man of boyish temper, as the potter remained. Sometimes, I think, he over-enjoyed himself. There was a tale how, returning one night, Mr. Smith fell to "chipping" the coach driver: "Here, you better let me take the reins. . . . Why, you ought to have your mother 'long with ye, to take care of ye." A week later, doing the same journey with the same driver, he fell asleep. Certainly the hour was late—near midnight; but probably he was also full of ale. At the alighting place the driver didn't awaken him. Instead, the man drove on for a mile or so, but then roused him to set him down. And when Mr. Smith began to curse he was told, "You en't fit to be trusted alone. You ought to have your mother 'long with ye, to take care of ye."

Moreover, his coach rides brought him into touch with the bigwigs of the neighbourhood; nay, visiting London oftener than they did, he was in some respects more of a man of the world. He knew what was going on as soon as the local squires. There is no doubt he was proud of his familiarity with the metropolis. Years afterwards, when his family trooped off, like all the rest of the world, to the Great Exhibition, he refused to join them. Now was the chance, and he took it, to play the superior person. "Can't see," he urged, "what you want to go to an exhibition for. Go and look in London shop windows"—that was exhibition enough, in his opinion.

It's not impossible, too, that his London acquaintances liked him for his own sake and found it worth while to cultivate pleasant relations with him for the sake of an occasional outing to his farm. They came down now and then for the coach ride, the landlord of the Angel at Islington being one who visited the potter-farmer at home several times.

Two customers were mentioned to me who once visited the farm, coming by coach, in response to an invitation; grave men, the farmer's seniors. In the afternoon they sang hymns—"God moves in a mysterious way" for one hymn. They sang with fervour, the farmer and his wife much approving, I gather.

CHAPTER XI

IN a gossip, one afternoon of heat and still sunshine, about the quantity of beer that countryfolk could put away with impunity if not even with benefit, so long as they kept on working, I heard a curious fact connected with the potteries at Farnborough and Cove. A bricklayer from Aldershot (before Aldershot Camp had been thought of) spent his time going from kiln to kiln, making good the damage caused by the great heat the kilns were subjected to. A giant man he was, beside whom a companion in our gossip—a man of thirteen stone or so—would have looked a child, it was said. This large-sized bricklayer's drink for the day was "half a bushel" provided for him. "But then, he worked for it." And very likely it was a hot job, in the kilns so seldom allowed to get cold. Hot or no, it was difficult for a man of his great size; he was hampered for room—could hardly turn round—inside the arches of the kiln. But he shaped them so finely that he had a reputation for them throughout the district. The fact is suggestive of the large number of potteries then working in the district. They kept a specialist employed at repairing their fabric. The man came to the Farnborough pottery about once a year, but I do not know for how many days.

More intimate with the land, more within the range of the potter's own close knowledge of the countryside, was the getting of fuel, for home use always, but especially for his pottery and afterwards for his daughter's bread oven too. Specialists, it's true—two experts, with special tools—were employed in the actual cutting of the turf; yet the rest of the work a man had to manage for himself, according to what he knew of the heaths and the boggy places, and the tracks over them, and where the wind and sun would help him or the rain hinder. A Gilbert White in that neighbourhood would have learnt many details about all such matters from a man like the potter, who had been as it were one of the fauna of the place, all his life. Not here, as in his farming, would William Smith make any blunders. I can fancy how he tramped over those open spaces, in the clear English air, with a sure eye for the weather and the soil, and an unhesitating confidence that he himself could get what he needed.

If properly cut, the best turf (as at Frimley Common) would grow so as to be fit for cutting again after five or six years. The harvest—it was a real harvest, as important to the potter as his hay or corn—was taken at midsummer, just when broad beans were in season. This gave a sort of perquisite: the turfcutters had a harvest supper of broad beans, at the farm. A bowl—"one of them great yellow bowls, you know"—was filled with well-cooked beans for them, and atop was put a lump of very fat bacon, the oil from which, trickling down, served better than butter.

After the turfs had been cut they were sometimes stacked up in little ricks on the common to dry, in which case the ricks were thatched. As the ashes from them made useful manure, farmers in the neighbourhood were wont to cart turf or peat to the cottagers for the sake of the ashes, which indeed had a market value of seven shillings the waggonload. On this account a fire was kept burning night and day at some cottages. Stacked up about six together—something like a child's card castle—the turfs made a glowing fire, and a very sweet-smelling one.

Not everybody might cut turfs: only "the privileged"—commoners, I suppose. Some jealousy was excited in the neighbourhood by a certain family—"a dirty lot"—who dwelt at the edge of Cove Common. They kept a few mares running about on the common; they reared a few colts and weaning calves. But they did not work; excepting that they cut much turf and wheeled it home in wheelbarrows, and, burning it, sold the ashes.

These details, perhaps, did not directly affect the

potter, unless as a feature of the provincial life he was himself so intimately a part of. His business brought him into direct personal touch with so much that was going on. The farm may have thrust him closer still; it doubtless gave him a more influential standing. But however that may have been, he came into contact, and on terms of hard necessity too, with all sorts and conditions of men, and had to hold his own amongst them.

For instance, the problem of fuel was only half solved after all when the turf harvest had been got in. He wanted wood too—cordwood and also sprays or bavins—and this involved business relations with the owners and purveyors of timber—squires, bailiffs, farmers—and some knowledge at least of the woodlands and the coppices. There were woods, and dealings over them, at Lady Palmer's at Farnborough Hill; others, belonging to Mr. Morant, the lord of the manor. A certain "old Farmer Nash," bailiff to the Dean of Chichester, supplied wood sometimes; sometimes, loppings from the fir-trees on the common were bought. For any timber served, although oak was preferred. The mainstay of the supply was perhaps from the Kelseys—a yeoman farmer family—who "had a lot of land" and with whom business seems to have fallen into a sort of routine. At any rate, on Boxing Day the Kelseys were wont to come to the farm to settle up accounts.

Years afterwards, when William Smith was dead, a letter which I saw lately from his widow to my father gave a touch of reality to this now forgotten business. The letter, undated, but written probably about 1875, requests my father to see Mr. Allden of Tongham (ah! I remember him) and pay him for five waggonloads of wood at sixteen shillings a load, and to state that no more would be wanted as the pottery was done with.

CHAPTER XII

THE farm never became, like the pottery, a subject of detailed and loving descriptions; but on the other hand, it provided a sort of atmosphere for all that was said about William Smith. It was a background: or, say, the whole background was enriched by it, whatever the subject of talk. Amidst incongruous matter—squires and rectors, village conditions, pigs, pottery, Christmas customs, the collecting of urine for steeping the seed wheat, the making of tinder and matches; and in chatter about the turnpike roads, and dog traction, and the to and fro of traffic between London and the far-off coast—from amidst and in and out of all this in its endless variety, farm words—single words such as glebe, harvest, thatching—sometimes glowed with a colour all their own, like ruddy sails on a summer evening sea. But the sea was the ancient country life and memory of an earlier era. The talk, indeed, took me back into George Borrow's time. And it seemed no mean or ugly country that I heard of. The farm—I think it must have been the farm—suggested dreams of quiet pastoral scenes, stately trees, great skies. In a word, the background was England—England in epitome; and showing up against it, yet a part of it too, sweated, stormed, frolicked like a boy at times, William Smith, potter: henceforth to be spoken of, oftener, as farmer. Large-limbed, full-blooded, probably grey before his time, he seems to need just such a background as the farm suggests. "I do wish I had got a photograph of him," exclaimed his last surviving daughter, with fond regret, for there is no portrait of the man left. "Such a big tall man," she went on, "and as straight as a dart." His head was big in proportion to his body, "and his stomach was sticking out, like." Several years later, recalling his "big face, rather florid," she repeated that he was "straight as a dart," adding that he "used to throw his shoulders back." If he was at all like his sons, as I have been assured he was, he had watchful grey eyes, full of kindly fun as a rule, though capable of kindling with sudden anger, and a mouth tender enough yet shaped by an inflexible doggedness of will.

Though inclined to be stout, he was none the less active, nay, joyously agile. Sometimes, when he reached home at night after a day in London, he would get his little children out of bed to dance reels with him on the bedroom floor. In the winter he was not above sliding, with other men, on a roadside pond: at one summer festivity—club feast or

cricket match—and probably at more than one, he
challenged anybody to jump backwards—or was it
over a chairback? So I was wrong to think of
him as an old countryman, as I habitually did. He
may have seemed like that when those who remembered their own childhood were picturing how
their father impressed them; but it is better to
fancy him almost youthful, on his coach rides and
pushing about London, or striding about his fields,
with the winter wind in his hair, or the strong July
sunshine pouring down on him.

For ordinary wear, on week-days, he had a white
" smock frock ": but on Sundays, or his visits to
London, he "got up" for the occasion, and was
something of a dandy in his countrified way. Top
boots (yellow tops, and the rest shining black),
knee breeches, longish drab waistcoat ("quite
drab") and frock-coat; with white kerchief round a
high white collar, and black beaver hat—oh, but
the farmer took a pride in his best clothes, as he
was well entitled to do, when one considers his
poverty-stricken childhood. Once, for some now
unknown reason, he had a white hat. The fur,
clipped off from the old hats, was held to be a good
thing to put on a cut finger. It was said that he
had to have his hats specially made for him in
London because of the great size of his head. But
I wonder. Where else was a countryman to get
a new beaver hat of any size, in those days? There

was no Aldershot town then. Farnham, a little lost place, was seven miles off: the farmer went to London oftener. Anyhow, he had a fine hat. The neckerchief he wore at the same time with it was wound twice round the neck and tied in a bow in front. His waistcoat had mother-of-pearl buttons. But all this gorgeousness was not for working days. On Monday mornings it was quite a business for the wife to get the farmer's best clothes (and later those of his two sons) down to the kitchen dresser to be brushed and folded for putting away.

Many years after he was dead and gone his son heard, and told me, a story of him which shows a little how he must have looked to others at this time—a substantial and stalwart man, standing up jolly and resolute in the farm places, a notable traveller by the London coach. It was at Aldershot station that the son, in his old age, fell into talk with a stranger, an oldish man, who looked like a farmer and claimed to have known all that district well in his younger days.

"I recollect once," the stranger said, "there was a stag from King William's hunt taken at some old farm or other out here and shut up in the buildin's until they could fetch it away. The cart come for'n from Windsor in the evenin'—about eight o'clock; and when we got there the old chap of the farm come out—looked as if he'd just come from London. He was in his top boots; and he'd had a drop. So we said we was come to fetch the deer. 'Deer?' he says. 'I en't goin' to bother about no deer to-night. You must come again for'n in the mornin'.' 'But 'tis King William's deer,' we says. 'I don't care whose deer 'tis,' he says, 'King William's or anybody else's. 'Tis too late to see about 'n to-night. You can't have 'n.' And we didn't have 'n, neither. But when we come for 'n next day the old chap was all right. He took us to some little pub or other and we had some drink and he was as jolly as anything."

The farmer's son related further that he heard this story, then said to the stranger, "I dessay you don't suppose that I knew that old chap. But I did; and I knowed where the deer was shut up, and all about it" (having peeped at the deer through a crack in the granary boards). "The old man was my father, and he'd just come off the coach from London."

As John Smith was barely four years old at King William's death, the above incident must have happened about 1836, when "the old" farmer was forty-six years old.

The farmer's daughter Ann had another picturesque memory of him, when she and her sisters were distressed—when their young lady aspirations were seriously hurt—by his uncouth manners; and this on Sunday evenings too. The way home from church was through a cornfield of their father's;

and despite his fine Sunday clothes the farmer could not be restrained from calling out, to scare the rooks and careless of the people, the magic word "Shuarlup." This occurs in a verse, sovereign against rooks:

" Shuarlup, shuarlup! You eats all the master's carn up!
'Tis but a little, and that's in the middle, Shuarlup!"

But the farmer was wont to scandalize his daughters by shouting the word with objurgations of his own against the rooks: "Shuarlup, you black sons of bitches!" "Whereupon," said his daughter, twinkling at last at the recollection, "we used to slink behind. Of course your mother and me was just of an age, and we felt it acutely. The rest of the people only laughed; but that made it worse."

Likely enough he was something of a "character." Mrs. Clayton once surprised him (but I wonder if he was really surprised, or only wished to humour her) singing pretty loudly, "Highty tighty, my man John," as he walked across one of his fields. "Well done, farmer!" she cried. He was a favourite with the gentry, and I dare say he knew how to please them. "Sarvant, sir," he would say, touching his hat respectfully, if meeting one of the local squires; but I can guess that the eyes were keen enough under the hat-brim, and that there was no bending of the back, "straight as a dart."

And no doubt he knew his own value in the

parish, knew that he was trusted more than others of his own standing. Moreover, even as an employer he was a man of some importance in that small community, if of none elsewhere. To the half-dozen men already employed at the pottery the farm added about five more.

Many more details on this level may be given— details about the village and the villagers, the local gentry and clergy, the farmhouse, the home interests, the family; and they all shed some light on William Smith and his strenuous career. Yet of his actual farming work little was ever told me, and that little only in passing, in reference to other matters.

Thus it was when the canal and the pottery were under discussion that I heard—just happened to hear—of a bargeload of potatoes (twelve tons, or perhaps twenty tons) being frozen into the canal for eight weeks, yet being eventually taken out unhurt. They had lain below the ice. This must have had to do with the farm; but it was not at all meant to be descriptive in that connection. More direct was a mention of mangold-growing, or another of pigs. I heard, in the most casual way, of the waggon team, of cows, of lambs. All put together, however, these details would hardly fill a page of this book; and they will be left there-fore to come into more appropriate place elsewhere.

CHAPTER XIII

THE NEIGHBOURHOOD

In trying to picture what Farnborough looked like
in those old days, I fancy that the details which
actually stir in my memory must have come in fact
not from Farnborough but from the woodland
pictures by Birket Foster and others in the maga-
zines, when I was still a little boy. The artist
supplied the details: it is sentiment that has put
them together for me into the fancy picture I call
Farnborough. But I think it true in essence for all
that. Sentiment has a way of picking out the
otherwise unnoticed values and thus finding the
deepest truths; and in this case I am persuaded
that the values of a vanished rural England are
precisely those which, above all others, ought to
be in any imaginary view of Farnborough in the
early half of the nineteenth century. Perhaps not
with exactly those curves, yet certainly with that
rich peacefulness, did the cornfields slope down
amongst bowery elm-trees to the village: certainly,
just in the manner the old pictures show, the far-
away hills and the rolling heaths lay under noble
clouds. In winter, whatever the cottage or the

103

H

lane, snow lay smooth on roof or hedgerow in the way everybody knows: bitter Christmas twilights, under gloomy skies, could not affect snowballing and could only heighten the promises of comfort from lit-up window or smoking chimney. Rural beauty, in short, and sturdy rustic cheerfulness, must be in any mental image of old Farnborough, to be correct. The picture should have a touch of the romantic and the sequestered: above all, it should suggest peacefulness, centuries old—peacefulness, and a quietness scarcely conceivable now. In those days there were no motors, no air-machines, no trains. I don't know how far the sound of threshing carried, from a barn. But I do know that the beat of horse hoofs in the distance, or the cries of a ploughman at work, or the far-off baying of a dog, cannot be called "noises" any more than the humming of bees can; yet there was nothing else to disturb the quiet of Farnborough. Nor is it safe to say that men like the farmers and peasants of England did not care for all this serenity and stillness that grew up with their own labours. Unawares, I think, their spirits absorbed it. I have been told that William Smith avoided Aldershot for the few years of his life after the Camp had broken up the silent heaths there. He never went near the place.

For all this, as his son John once reminded me, we shouldn't care to go back to those old times.

Whatever its romantic charm, whatever beauty
sentiment may have felt to be present in it, Farnborough village had squalid features, noisome not
to the eye alone. Modern tastes could not have
endured it. On either side of the "street" was an
open ditch or drain, in which the sewage was
often stagnant. The "old pollard" was the scene
for pig-killings—including those from Street Farm
itself. Straw fires to singe the slaughtered pigs
were built, in public, under the old tree. Somewhere near here stood probably the village stocks,
not quite disused, even at that date.

Imagine a modern motorist coming on any of the
village excitements it is easy to picture to oneself in
such connections! But at least there was no motor
noise. Very few people were about. In the "old
pollard" just mentioned owls nested. They greeted
the boys who climbed after them with weird noises,
"like a cat miawling," and with a fierce defence
that made the adventure a risky one. Most people
kept pigs, and made a practice of opening the pigsties every morning and letting the occupants out
into the village street for the day. There can
hardly have been any pretty front gardens. Pigs
browsed on the grass that grew by the open drain.
"Old Sally Bridger" kept ducks and "a lag of
geese," which also frequented the street. "They
might as well; for there wasn't nobody else."

No: there was nobody else. There was no

Aldershot Camp; no railway. The turnpike road with the stage-coaches came little nearer than a mile away. The church, the rectory, sundry big houses of the gentry, lay aloof on the gentle hills or in fenced parks; here and there other lost villages occupied spots of fertility in the wide heath country; but, like them, Farnborough kept to itself. It had little intercourse with the outer world. Now and again the silence would be broken by some farm waggon on the road, by some shouting horde of children, by the footsteps of some solitary wayfarer; but on the whole a peace undisturbed for ages lay on the village; and the village people—oblivious of the peace as fish are oblivious of the water they swim in—had nothing to interest them but one another's affairs. Here Farmer Smith carried on his pottery business, managed his farm, his pigs and cows and horses, his hay and corn, and became incidentally, as will be told, the rector's right-hand man; here he brought up his family; here he took care of his relatives—not his wife's, but his own; who may now be spoken of, as illustrating how parochial his environment was, for all his experience of London. Truly the village was slow to understand what was going on elsewhere. Long after the farmer's death his eldest son William, it was said, was terribly scared by the coming of the ordnance surveyors: he took them to be Fenians. And that must have been twenty-five years later than the period to be dealt with now, when Farmer Smith was still at the zenith of his career.

Himself the oldest of the family, he got his two brothers into his pottery as soon as possible. His wife is said to have esteemed them, as sensible young men. But when still young they died—both of them—of diabetes within a few days of one another. This curious thing is told of them lying dead: corruption followed so slowly that their burial was deferred for a month. A fear of premature burial lingered in that family into the present century.

Besides the two brothers, William Smith had three sisters, not so well spoken of—Elizabeth, Ann, and Fanny. The last named became a laundress, married a man in London and was early widowed; Ann seems to have made a bad marriage; while of the third, "Aunt Bet," various things are told. These three women, not living at Farnborough, came at rare intervals to visit their old mother; and though they contributed but little to her keep they did not scruple to grumble at what their brother the farmer was doing for her. This may have been serviceable in a way neither they nor he realized, for it provided a vent for his temper. Exasperated he often was by his father-in-law, old Blackburn, at the farm: but he could not afford to let loose his annoyance in that quarter. On the other hand, he was under no obligation to

spare his sisters; and there is reason to think he let
them know it sometimes.

They gave him provocation enough. Ann's bad
marriage was a thorn in the flesh. It must have
been known in the village that Farmer Smith had
a disgraceful brother-in law. And sometimes this
man was seen approaching while the family was at
dinner. I can picture the meal in the old farm
kitchen: the children with their backs to the
window; the farmer facing it where he could see
what was going on outside, and seeing—the
drunken shame. Then he would exclaim to the
children, "Don't go to the door! Don't look out
o' the window!"

Yet it may be supposed that the offence to his
pride was not so irritating as the pinpricks that
came from Aunt Bet. She had married a man at
Sunninghill, and been left a widow, with ten
children. As caretaker and pew-opener at the
church she got a respectable living, I suppose, and
she seems to have fancied herself. "Used to walk
about the farm—she did—picking up her skirts and
angling out her elbows, as if the place wasn't good
enough for her," the farmer would comment
bitterly, expecting, perhaps, to hear further of this
offence from his own wife. But his worst irritation
of all, because so trivial and so unnecessary, came
from his sister's calling him "brother," and that,
too, in so affected a voice as almost to drop the

"r." Any Hampshire man—and the farmer was all Hampshire—will feel the enormity of that offence, like a criticism of his county.

Yet the relations between brother and sister were not always unhappy. In eating broad beans, while one of them—the farmer, I think—liked the tough husk of the bean the other preferred the mealy inner part. So, when this food was on the table (to think of it is to think of midsummer and the welcome coolness of the old kitchen), the two would sit next one another so that the one could, between thumb and finger, pinch out the soft inside of the beans on to the other's plate. A custom, this, it may be surmised, reminiscent, even then, of an earlier period and a still more unsophisticated village life, when the brother and sister were children together in their mother's cottage at Cove.

In contemplating that mother, an old woman by now, whom her son was taking care of in a cottage near his pottery at Farnborough, and whom Aunt Bet with all her offensive airs and graces came to see —in contemplating that mother one gets back into a period almost incredibly distant, and into a village life very remote, yet not incompatible with the neighbourhood which was the farmer's very home.

CHAPTER XIV

DAME SMITH

IT has been already told how William Smith's mother was left a widow with six children when he, the eldest of the children, was but eleven years old; and how, upon his taking the potshop at Farnborough, he got her to make a home for him at a cottage there. What her age was has not been told; but she can hardly have been less than fifty at the time of her son's second marriage, when he went to live at the farm; and at fifty she may very well have been near to old age, for village women grow old soon, if they are poor and hardworking. And Dame Smith (I never heard her Christian name) was both.

Charwoman she had been at Farnborough Park, at first for Squire Wilmot, and then for his successor, Mr. Morant — not called "Squire" to me. She was able to bring home food from the kitchen at the great house, where she worked daily. But it may be supposed that easier times for her soon followed her entry into the potshop cottage, or at any rate her son's removal to the farm. Her family was off her hands: at the potshop a caretaker would be handy: and who so eligible as this stark old woman?

Moreover, she worked for the farm family. Until the children there had begun to grow up the grandmother baked all the farmhouse bread in her oven at the potshop cottage. The farmer's eldest daughter Susan helped at this; the younger girls having to carry up the grist from the farm and bring back the loaves, on a little toy go-cart of their brother's. A week's supply of bread was made in a batch. I can't say whether Dame Smith was paid in money or in kind. It was the custom daily to send her dinner along from the farm, with half a pint of beer—no more, "because she was very fond of her beer," the farmer's daughter Ann said many years afterwards, recalling frequent errands to carry the old woman's dinner.

And baking for the farm family wasn't all. Dame Smith baked for sale, as I will tell; and every week (not oftener?) a special loaf for Lady Palmer of Farnborough Hill was baked on the open hearth, in an earthenware dish with an earthenware bowl turned over it. Once a year, also, a great batch of buns was made at the cottage for the boys' feast at Mr. Green's school.

But what of the bread that was sold? Well, Dame Smith once kept a shop in that potshop cottage. Such a shop! Groceries, brought all the way from Farnham, seven miles away—by what conveyance I don't know—were sold there; rice, ginger—but I have with my own eyes seen at least the drawers some of the shop commodities were kept in; for eventually a counter for the larger shop at the farm—that counter with the caraway-seed and scoop of my childish memories—was fashioned from the shop fittings in Dame Smith's cottage.

But it puzzles me to guess what sort of trade the old lady can have done: it's easier to imagine how lonely, how silent the little shop must have been, with sunshine sleeping in the window, flies buzzing, and the smell of new loaves. Perhaps a potter came in sometimes, or a child specially sent. But there cannot have been any casual customers. The outside public can hardly have known there was a shop at all. The window of it was at the back, looking out upon no thoroughfare, but on the pottery kiln: for the shop was not in the front of the cottage, towards the road; nor was the cottage itself even on the road. It lay aside, fifty or a hundred yards away. Intending customers had to climb a stile, walk down a garden or field path, and through the kitchen, before they could find themselves in Dame Smith's shop.

Of the kitchen there is a pencil drawing—or rather, the kitchen hearth, with the old lady sitting beside it. A few other details have been remembered, about the cottage interior. On one side of

DAME SMITH

the hearth was room for a stool; the other side was built out to form a chimney-corner seat, "wide enough for two children." A lazy place, this was, where it was too dark to see to do anything, where all one could do was to sit and talk and keep warm. On the wall beside the hearth hung three shelves holding china. Under this was the copper lid of a large copper caldron. The lid, highly polished, made a handsome wall ornament. Near to it was a piece of needlework, on silk. The farm children, if not others, called it "The Queen of Sheba"; but it represented, against a background of leaves, a lady in a tall black hat, something like a man's hat. On the recesses of the shelves, when the shop had been given up and the groceries removed, a set of crockery was kept which may be spoken of again. Mention has already been made of the lead stored in the cottage, for glazing the ware at the pottery.

"A cawnayin' old woman"—that is how John Smith described his grandmother in after years— a false sort of old woman, obsequious and pious to please the rich, disagreeable to all others. Evidently her grandson didn't like her. Yet Dame Smith had had a hard time of it and may be excused if she did indeed go out of her way to make well-to-do folk think her amiable and good. As for her being disagreeable—the children who so remembered her may have been a little to blame themselves.

Said another grandchild—it was Ann—" We children used to torment her so. She used to burn ' scrabble,' if you know what that is. Fir-pins. Of course they burnt a lot of fir-wood at the pottery; and grandmother used to have big fires of these (fir-pins) tossed up behind a block of wood. She had a stick for a poker; and we used to get the stick on fire at the end and whirl it round in the air to look like a ribbon: Grandmother'd get so cross—but we didn't care. I'm afraid we was very naughty. We were sent up there to be company for her; but that's how we behaved."

Yet if children were occasionally tiresome, the main tenor of the old woman's life was probably most tranquil in that cottage, with young folk to chatter to her in the dark chimney corner, or with her own scrubbing and baking to occupy her, amid the fragrance of "scrabble" burning, and of newly baked bread. For if ill-temper had been the rule, the gusts of it, as if disturbing an habitual calm, would not have been clearly remembered after many years. One or two such occasions there were, however.

An ill-timed visit from Mrs. Clayton, the rector's wife, was the cause of one disturbance. The farm children had but just brought the dinner along, when Mrs. Clayton came in. Promptly Dame Smith caught up the dinner and hid it under her apron—as if not wishing to appear too well off. But she had not been quick enough. "What have you got there?" asked the visitor; nor would she be put off until her curiosity was satisfied. And how angry was the farmer when he heard of this affair. There must have been a storm, that day, in his mother's cottage.

Another time it was the old woman herself who lost her temper—when she was asked to sit for the pencil portrait of her. "What a temper she was in, when Miss Murray came!" exclaimed her grand-daughter Ann, in reminiscence. Miss Murray came from Frimley; and that is all I know about the artist. It may be fairly surmised that ladies of leisure, like Miss Murray and Mrs. Clayton, were not very easily tolerated in hard-working homes, and not the more so because they had to be treated with some obsequiousness.

Galling the gay spirits of a woman like Mrs. Clayton must have been; especially galling to the poor and old, because of the implied superiority, the kindly patronage the lady affected, as if people like Mrs. Smith were dolls for her amusement. It would not surprise me (yet I shall never know now) to learn that Miss Murray had been instigated to go to her portrait-drawing by silly talk of Mrs. Clayton's. It must have been from herself that the latter was known to have considered Dame Smith the "handsome" old lady of the parish, while Dame Maynard (or was it Dame Saxby?) was the "pretty" one.

There was quite a colony of old widow women living at or around the pottery, and all called "Dame" this or that. Besides those already named were Dame Trusler and Dame Cook. Dame Saxby lived next door to Dame Smith. Dame Trusler "was a little old woman," who wore caps like her neighbour's in the picture—caps edged with velvet bands. Once she was curious to know how she looked in her cap when she was eating; and she got a looking-glass and set it before her at dinner, so as to see for herself.

CHAPTER XV

SQUIRES

I am sorry I can find no memoranda of a certain talk, in which it was told how ruin, overtaking one of the leading families in Farnborough, ended in the sale of their house and the final carving up of their estate into building plots by "land butchers" —that is to say, by speculating agents, who bought the estate for that purpose. There had been a scandal, so the tale went—a divorce, I think; and the history of the property, never passing to a second generation of owners but going from hand to hand until the land butchers got it at last, was given to me in illustration of a theory to the effect that ruin always overtook a house, whoever owned it, which had been disgraced by anything so scandalous as a divorce. And the want of any record of this theory is what I regret; for it seemed to me a sort of folk-theory. Certainly it may have prevailed in Farmer Smith's family alone—a phase of their rather puritanical attitude—but I got the impression that provincials in general shared that view; that their deep respect for "the gentry" delegated to Providence the national duty of keeping the gentry in order. On these terms individual backslidings in the upper classes might be safely deprecated, yet left alone; on these terms it was possible to hold an individual lady or gentleman in light esteem without imperilling the whole fabric of English society.

So the gentry were left to go their own way. Farnborough folk troubled little about them, save in as far as business contact with them could not be avoided. This, I suppose, was mutual. At any rate Farmer Smith had other matters, other people, to attend to, and the names of his social superiors only emerged from the talk about him in much the same way as the larger houses stand up here and there in a wide landscape. The leisured classes had just that value. One cannot picture old Farnborough without the local squires, and something should be said about them before we get back to the more intimate and necessary life of the village and the working folk. In the woodland England one has to imagine — a heathland England too, round about Farnborough—the country seats of the gentry nestle in their parks in a sort of silvery summer light, far spread, beautiful in its dim suggestion of the land under it.

Spread over the country far and wide, with comfort and leisure, the bigwigs, it must be thought, had still but a dull time of it. They were too far and wide. Even they could not go to

London often. The coach roads afforded them no
sufficient means of intercourse, though it's pleasant
to picture those great ways linking town to town,
park to park. At Farnborough at any rate there
was next to no hunting, next to no game preserv-
ing. The gentry didn't know what else to do with
themselves; so they gambled. Half a dozen names
(but I will not repeat them) were mentioned to me
in this connection: half a dozen estates throughout
Hampshire and Surrey were cited as having been
impoverished by the reckless dissipation of their
owners, bored to death. The smaller fry followed
the fashionable lead. A sort of yeoman squires
gambled away their all—even their prospective
crops. And badly hit they were if after all their
crops failed—their wheat, their barley.

Little enough can be told of these people. Mr.
Currie, of Minley Hall, used always to buy some of
the Welsh sheep that were brought that way
periodically. Squire Timm—he who sent down
furniture from Somerset House by the returning
pottery waggon—had a model farm and showed
the Farnborough folk what a crop of mangold
could be like. Squire Tickell and another (Squire
Laurel, I think), returning from London on the
same coach with Farmer Smith, derided him for
an ignorant and credulous fellow, because he told
them that the new railway (the South-Western) was
to be carried across Fleet Pond; where in fact it

I

may be seen to this day. These, with others who might be named, lived too far away for Farnborough to know or care much about them. The only local grandees were Lady Palmer and Mr. Morant.

Lady Palmer has been mentioned several times and there is but little more worth saying about her now. Her bailiff, old Farmer Nash, may be spoken of later on. She was not the owner, but only the tenant, of Farnborough Hill—now the ex-Empress Eugénie's. The property, at that time, was copyhold of the Manor of Farnborough, the holder of it (non-resident) being the Dean of Chichester. When the Dean died, the lord of the manor, Mr. Morant, caused his steward to seize the best horse in the Dean's stables as a heriot. The right being thus asserted, the horse was paid for.

It was Lady Palmer, or a friend of hers, who, missing the expected curtsey from Farmer Smith's second daughter, went to the farmhouse to complain. "She couldn't think what had come over Ellen—such a nice girl. But——" How the interview went I never heard; but after it Ellen gave out that she wasn't going to curtsey to Lady Palmer. I can believe that she never did; she was my own mother. Her elder brother William had a tender reflected interest in Lady Palmer; he married a maid of her ladyship's—a cook, I should infer from an old manuscript book of recipes that has been preserved. As for Farmer Smith himself,

I am unaware that his life touched Lady Palmer's
in any other way than in the occasional purchase
of bavins from her woods.

Mr. Morant, the lord of the manor, owner of
Farnborough Park and of William Smith's farm,
was not quite such a negligible quantity. It's true,
business with him seems to have been carried on
through his steward, Mr. Kininment, and Mr.
Morant's own relations with the farmer went no
farther than sending him a present of rooks at rook-
shooting time. He probably never knew how little
his civility was appreciated. The farmer not only
disliked rook-pie himself, he also refused to pass
the gift on to any of his customers. People in
London might have been glad to have rooks; but
William Smith caused them to be buried, holding
them to be "poisonous" food. They are, I am
told, very bitter to the taste, needing to be skinned.
Only the breasts are fit to be eaten.

Yet Mr. Morant's presence was felt all through
the parish. It was his wife (no doubt with his
consent and perhaps with his help) who started
and supported the best school in the village; it must
have been Mr. Morant who was the chief pillar of
the church. In his park, and near his mansion,
stood the ancient parish church. The rectory lay
under his eye, across a lane: the rector was his
nearest neighbour. The first railway couldn't cross
Farnborough without crossing his land. In short,

nothing of a public nature could go on in the village without Mr. Morant's knowledge; little or nothing could be done without his consent.

At church one of the chief attractions for the school children was to see the Morant family come in. This weekly event has been described by the farmer's daughter Ann, who seems to have gone to church with the other children then, as if from a Sunday-school. The church being in Mr. Morant's own park, Mr. Morant of course had his special pew, probably screened off. And when Mr. Morant came in, all the congregation, or at least all the children, were wont to stand up. "There was Mr. Owey, and Mr. Harry," besides two other sons and a daughter, but "No; we didn't stand up for them. But then old Morant would come in," stumpingly, I gathered, from the accents of the talk just then. And as he appeared the schoolmistress's forefinger would shoot upright and all the schoolchildren got to their feet. Best of all, however, they enjoyed the occasional appearances of a nephew—Captain something or other. "They said he weighed sixteen stone." The children watched eagerly for him. "Miss Morant was the most lovely girl" the farmer's daughter ever saw. There is a low stool in my possession—a neat enough little bit of furniture, bought, I suppose, at the final dispersal of the Morant household—which is said to have been Miss Morant's, used by her when she was having her

MISS MORANT

hair dressed. It suggests the comelier side of the
gentlefolks' life.

The Dean of Chichester, though non-resident, was
of importance enough to lend respectability in
Farnborough to the Church of England. Owner
of Farnborough Hill and landlord to Lady Palmer,
he was also uncle to Mr. Green — a man much
looked up to in the parish, not so aloof as the landowners, yet one of their class for all that.

It was Mr. Green who supported for many years
a school for boys in Farnborough—a really good
school, considering all things—more than a cut
above any Board-school. Farmer Smith's sons
were amongst the scholars—a pair of old copybooks
of the elder of them show a careful copying out of
modern verse (a poem of Tennyson's included), and
so were two of his grandsons. For Mr. Green
lived to a goodly age. He had been an officer—a
subaltern—at Waterloo; wounded, and crippled for
life, in that battle.

CHAPTER XVI

THE ANCIENT OUTLOOK

WHAT little civilization there was in the parks and homes of the gentry filtered lazily down upon the working folk of the neighbourhood, through the rectories of Farnborough, Frimley, and Hawley. No powerful Dissenting organization quickened it, and it did not get far. The near village of Cove hardly felt any influence from it; and that is an interesting point in connection with Farmer Smith, seeing that he had been born and brought up in Cove.

According to the farmer's daughter Ann the people of that benighted parish were more uncouth, more countrified in manners and talk, than those of Farnborough, two miles away. And Ann's brother John said, "The Cove people weren't exactly heathens," but there was no place of worship for them to go to nearer than Farnborough Church in the squire's park. Eventually a number of seats were reserved there for Cove. But only the women availed themselves of that privilege. The men didn't go to church.

What the people did go to was a funeral. "The

Cove funerals were rather noted," said the farmer's daughter quoted above. "Mother used to talk about 'em. I suppose father knew all about 'em, but she (being of Westminster) had never seen anything like it, and she used to laugh. . . . I remember her telling especially about the funeral of a man named Matthews. He was some connection of father's, I think. He had a little property, and was a good deal respected. Everybody went to *his* funeral. And they hollered and shouted—got on chairs and called out like he used to at hunting, to the dogs. 'Yoicks, my dogs! Yoicks, my dogs!' They went through all his life like that. . . . Your grandmother used to laugh so. . . ."

And the Hawley people—they too laughed, or at any rate were glad over these peculiarities of Cove, valuing a good Cove funeral above several weddings, on account of the trade it brought into their village. For Hawley seems to have been the burial-ground for Cove. And many bearers (two dozen, I think) were needed, for carrying a corpse all those miles.

"Uncouth"—yes, that word will fit Cove; and if the surrounding parishes, blessed with more squires and parsons, found it well to be rather less noisy, it is not clear that they had reason to plume themselves on any other superiority. There may have been, and I incline to think there were, scattered households with an outlook to have pleased a

Wesley, perhaps even a Wordsworth—germs, these, of a civilization that is springing up all over England to-day; but, in Farmer Smith's youth, however tender and quiet individual tastes may have been here and there, the general temper of the neighbourhood was bucolic—was grossly materialistic.

The clergy do not appear to have done much to correct this, even by force of example. One rector of Farnborough was named to me whose life was little short of a public scandal, doctor of divinity though he was. He got into the clutches of moneylenders; he was a drunkard; finally he was excommunicated. So, when he died, his place of burial was not told. But old people claimed to know where it was, and not the old only. "I've jumped over his grave many a time," said the farmer's son John, "when I was a boy."

A successor of this ne'er-do-well doctor of divinity was at any rate no spendthrift. He married a rich wife, much younger than himself. "He christened her; and he married her." Yet wherever else he laid up treasure, it can hardly be said to have been in the affection or the esteem of his parishioners.

Then there was a neighbour—the rector of Cove, I was told, but I think this must have been a mistake —who earned a sort of respect, but not on clerical grounds. This gentleman, like Squire Currie of

Minley, was a regular buyer of Welsh sheep. "He used to have 'em killed two at a time." He was a one-armed man, and when the butcher came to kill the sheep, the reverend gentleman "would run 'em down and catch 'em—because he was such a beggar to run."

In these circumstances primitive pagan beliefs were slow to die out, if they didn't exactly flourish. It is likely that people suffered in their wits—were sluggish, I mean, and as credulous as they were densely ignorant—for want of plentiful and brisk social intercourse. There were no railways, or newspapers, or telegrams. All that people could know of one another or of an outside world was what was passed on in gossip and rumour. The population was very sparse. Wild and lonely heaths made much of its habitat; what wonder then that it hardly got away from ancient—almost prehistoric—explanations of things, or from silly tales? Will-o'-the-wisps, fairies, witches, all gave ocular proof of their existence: ghosts were not unknown. Charms, prognostications, seemed truer than Gospel truth.

Born and brought up in this atmosphere, William Smith was far too sympathetic and normal a man to escape its influence. I will not say that he exactly believed any of this primitive lore; but his childlike mind accepted it. Like a sensible man he accommodated himself to it; or he passed it on for what it might be worth. A little of it—only a very little, and I wish it was more—came trickling down to me.

I heard two items about fairies. In one, it was told how two fairies, wanting to cross the brook, could not face the running water, so mounted the backs of two calves grazing in the pasture near by. In this way, the first fairy was able to cross. But the second, over-elated, cried out in the middle, "Well done, my little calf," and was immediately pitched off into the stream.

The second item was not a tale. It gave the usual explanation of a ring of darker grass in the plat at back of the farmhouse: fairies dancing had left that mark. The interesting thing about it, to me, is the impression I got (it was from Ann) that this was not the work of numerous gossamer hordes as in "A Midsummer-Night's Dream." Only five or six fairies danced around the ring at Farnborough, and they were biggish fellows, four feet high or so. I know no justification for picturing them, as nevertheless I do, as tough, leathery, wizened with age, mocking and unhuman in expression. Their size, on the other hand, seems to have been suggested to me; and it would suit the two fairies in the calf-riding story.

John Smith, when asked about witches, admitted that he had never known one: yet his reply suggested that some belief in them was common in his boyhood and that his father the farmer neither doubted nor disapproved of them. There were, in fact, some very queer old women about, one of whom, Honour Willett by name, was a wart charmer. One of the farmer's daughters had recourse to Honour Willett's help. Another of these queer old women—her surname not recorded—had the same Christian name. Queerness was, perhaps, her worst fault: there is no accusation of witchcraft against her. She used to keep little sucking pigs, rearing them by spoon-feeding. And Mr. Smith, who had a largish number of pigs, would often have one over—one too many in the farrow. Then he would say, "Take it over to Old Honour." The little pigs soon learned to follow her about as if they were dogs.

And then there were ghosts—at least there was one ghost. That phantom I spoke of in an earlier chapter as a witch was, I learnt afterwards, the ghost of old Mr. Barnes, the previous tenant of Street Farm. He it was who used to sit all alone on a field-gate o' dark nights, with no head.

The farmer's daughter Ann once repeated to me a verse:

> "Three old women tied up in a apple-tree—
> Hung all the week and cut down on a Saturday."

As this may have come from her Yorkshire connections, and not from Farnborough, not much should be made of it here. Yet the touch of savagery in it is suggestive of traditions not out of keeping with the more sinister aspects of the heathland that surrounded Farnborough. More certainly at home there, more surely characteristic of the neighbourhood, was a creepy tale that Spring-heeled Jack was about. His macabre figure haunted the place for years: he was still at his insane tricks, even in my own memory; frightened women had seen him.

Truly the general outlook was medieval, though by no means invariably to be deprecated therefore. One pleasant custom was as follows: at pig-killing (an interesting occasion at some time or other in almost every cottage) the forechine was salted and put by for a special event, if there were prospects of such an event in a family sufficiently soon. It was a sort of traditional celebration; guests at a time of childbirth were regaled on forechine. Perhaps after all it was but a passing fashion in this little group of villages. On the other hand, it sounds like a bit of magic surviving from pre-Christian ages.

And there was another survival from pre-Reformation days. Farmer Smith would have been horrified at the hint of anything papistical about him; yet this was a nightly prayer of his:

"Four corners to my bed;
Four angels round my head;
Matthew, Mark, Luke, and John,
Bless the bed that I lie on."

Whence had he got it? He must have learnt it in his childhood, before the eighteenth century was over. But to speculate about its emergence in that Cove Cottage is to begin dreaming of a rugged population living and dying, half lost in the heathland, as long ago as Henry VIII., or as when, say, the fresco, lately uncovered, was painted in Farnborough parish church.

CHAPTER XVII

RECTORS

But about the time of William Smith's second marriage a more enlightened influence, in the person of a kindlier rector—Mr. Eckersell—was beginning to be felt in Farnborough; and it happened that the new Mrs. Smith was of a temper to welcome the new force and to work with it.

Susannah Blackburn, it may be recalled, had been brought up at Westminster, near to the Abbey, and she had been to a boarding-school. It has been told too how she helped her husband with the invoices of his pottery-ware, and how she enabled him, thanks to her father's money, to take Street Farm. And as she began, so she went on. Without ever trying to take the first place, she stood behind her husband's every effort, co-operating with it. Not only did she put her own education at his service; she did something towards imparting some of it to him. His schooling, remember, had lasted but three days; but, thanks to his wife, he learnt to read a little. Not much. His practical life, with so many interests and duties, cannot have left him much time, or perhaps much energy, for book-learning. Still, somehow or other, by the time his children were old enough to notice such things, he could manage to read Bible or Prayer-Book. One or the other (each has been mentioned) lay always beside his desk, in the corner of the kitchen partitioned off for his office—his " shop," as he called it. The volume, whichever it was, was printed with the long " s," which to modern eyes looks so much like " f."

Quietly, without any parade of doctrine, Mr. Eckersell seems to have made his way to his villagers' hearts and to have mollified their manners. Probably my opinion of him is coloured in his favour by the strong regard that was felt for him at Street Farm; yet other people, outside the farmhouse, felt it too. I think the man liked his parishioners, was genuinely interested in their affairs, took pleasure in their pleasures, and listened to the wisdom of his own pure human kindness in suggesting little improvements here and there, or in bringing good-temper into their normal festivities. Was he not present—I think he must have been: it sounds so much like a Sunday-school jollification—on the day of that cricket-match between Mr. Morant's men from Farnborough Park and Farmer Smith's men from his pottery and farm; when the farmer, in such merry spirits, was challenging a neighbour to jump backwards? True, an unseemly fight occurred, between Mr. Smith's son William and another boy; and when some of the neighbours, scandalized, cried shame on the farmer for not parting the combatants, he said, "No. Let 'em fight it out. Then if one of 'em gets beat they won't want to fight again." No doubt the rector was absent from this distressing scene; but I feel equally without doubt that the whole day's affair had his countenance. It is so easy to picture him beaming upon his parishioners at play in the great man's park, on a hot summer day under elm-trees.

For, be it repeated, Mr. Eckersell warmly liked his flock and admired many of their doings. A great supporter, he was, of the village club, and attended the yearly club-feast at the "Ship." He attended other feasts—harvest suppers especially—"wherever they were respectable." In this connection there is odd confirmation of Mr. Eckersell's interest in the village life. Farmers, in his days, were very nearly self-supporting; I mean, their own produce went a long way towards meeting their own needs. For the harvest supper at any substantial farm the farmer would kill a pig, or a calf, or a sheep, and take pride in having the table supplied wholly with food from the farm. And Mr. Eckersell urged Mr. Smith to go farther still. At his instigation (possibly the farmer privately damned a little at the troublesome fad) some of the crockery for the harvest supper was made at

Mr. Smith's own potshop. The clay cannot have been good enough for it all—or the handiwork neat enough, perhaps. Plates and dishes were made, however, and pint cups and half-pint cups. When not in use the things were stowed away in Dame Smith's cottage, on a shelf she had once used for storing goods, when she kept shop.

Some papers lately put into my hands show an unexpected friendship between the rectory and Street Farm, which possibly explains Farmer Smith's nickname, "Bishop." Several letters are amongst the papers. They are not all dated; but one of them, containing congratulations to Mrs. Smith on the birth of a fine baby girl, with references to the two elder children, is dated November, 1830, when Mr. Eckersell was at the most prosperous tide of his career. One letter from him to Mrs. Smith (it would have been useless to write to her unschooled husband), is a request that "Smith" will superintend various diggings and manurings at the rectory garden during the rector's absence; and gives instructions for planting tulips, hyacinths, and anemones. In another, probably a draft, Mrs. Smith respectfully informs the rector of collecting the tithes. "Smith" has got them all in save from two neighbours, who "hadn't even the civility to take the least notice" of the request; and Smith has presided at a customary dinner (at the "Ship," the rector had suggested) to all who had paid, as

K

well as to various esteemed churchgoers, not
property-owners or tithe-payers. The letter states
that they all enjoyed themselves and went home in
good time (a happy thing, that!); and it ends with
a statement of the moneys received and the balance
in hand, " which Smith will pay in to Wright's Bank
in London to-morrow, as he has to go to London."

When the Eckersells left Farnborough, some
nine years later, their goods were packed for them
by the farm folk and sent to London—probably in
the waggon that commonly took pottery-ware.
There is, in Mrs. Smith's neat handwriting, a
longish inventory of the packing-cases and their
contents, including " 2 Targetts, Bows, and Stands,"
suggestive of archery parties with the gentry (Miss
Morant, perhaps), and "11 Hampers with Wine,"
suggestive of poor Mr. Eckersell's downfall. And
another piece in Mrs. Smith's handwriting is the
draft of an address presented to the beloved rector,
together with a testimonial subscribed for by his
parishioners, when he went away. There is also
the draft of a petition to the Bishop on Mr. Eckersell's behalf. I don't know whether it was ever
presented. It is pretty clear that the farmer's wife
was the leading spirit in the parish all through this
heartburning affair of the rector's departure—
probably she was the best educated of all the
villagers; and I have not much doubt that throughout it all she was mindful of her husband's interests.

By the end of Mr. Eckersell's ministry William
Smith was no longer the unimportant potter
Susannah Blackburn had married. She was making
of him one of the leading farmers of the neighbourhood. But he was himself a popular man;
and it is likely that the whole parish was really
softened in its manners by the good relations Mrs.
Smith did so much to foster between her husband
and the rector. It might be considered, I at least
should consider it, "toadying" to-day: but the
times are altered. There is no reason to suppose
that there was anything but devout sincerity in
Mrs. Smith's professed respect for Mr. Eckersell.

The next rector, Mr. Clayton, would possibly
have left a bigger mark if he had come after a less
popular man. As it is, my impression paints him
as wealthily indolent, aloof from his parishioners.
Very likely I am wrong. In the only detail I have
got of any talk about him, he figures as a landowner, encouraging the cultivation of mangold.
This preceded Squire Timm's demonstration, already
mentioned. The very first mangolds ever grown
in Farnborough were introduced by Mr. Clayton as
an experiment, on the glebe he had rented to
Farmer Smith. And this is really all I know about
Mr. Clayton.

His wife, on the other hand, has been mentioned
to me over and over again, usually with an air of
asking toleration for the silliness of a thoroughly

well-meaning and generous woman. The villagers
seem to have loved Mrs. Clayton in spite of themselves, notwithstanding the shocks their prejudices
often had from her. A comely woman she was—
she weighed eighteen stone — good-tempered,
frivolous, possibly bored to death for something to
do in that slow place. She seems to have invented
a sort of district visiting for her own entertainment, looking upon the villagers as amusing pets.
How she treated the old dames who lived near Mr.
Smith's potkiln has been told; and that was typical.
The puzzled old people cannot have known quite
what to make of Mrs. Clayton. There was "Old
Six O'Clock" for instance. I venture to guess that
the lady herself, who found this name for him, gave
it in appreciation of his upright and downstraight
character. However that may be, she wrote a little
book about him, with that for its title, and was fool
enough to let it get about the village. Greatly
offended was the old man when he found out about
it; and indeed the boys used to tease him with his
new nickname. And how was he to guess that the
lady meant nothing unkind to him, but badly
wanted some occupation for her own nimble wits?
Or how was she to guess, for that matter, that
mere cottage people have any sensitiveness? Even
to this day, seventy years later, district visitors
don't always understand it.

Mrs. Clayton, none the less, was clever enough

to have known better, had she only thought. A clever, extravagant, and fashionable woman, she took a real delight in lovely things, and in skilful work. I have told how she fashioned special shapes for pottery. She it was, too, who introduced more lavish decorations into Farnborough Church for festival seasons. At home her garden was a joy: in the village school—and this was a momentous thing—she reached the children's taste in a direction new to them. For one day she brought in some "fairy cups"—the small scarlet fungi sometimes found in winter hedgerows; and offered a reward for others of them—so dainty. Was ever such a thing heard of before in that village?

In their slovenly medieval manner the people no doubt had a traditional eye for beauty. But it had to be useful too, and what their forefathers had cared for. Now, though, something else was stirring: villagers were beginning to feel, to taste, to admire, for themselves. I don't suggest that Mrs. Clayton originated this change; but at least she appealed to it, when she got the schoolchildren to search for "fairy cups" for her.

CHAPTER XVIII

SCHOOLS

I.—Mrs. Cooke's

At one of the queer little Farnborough schools there was, I dimly remember hearing, a boy with a white patch in his hair, which the parson told him Providence had set there for a mark to identify him if he should ever commit a crime. "And did he?" I asked. No; he never did. "Providence," John Smith (who told me) reflected in his dry whimsical way—"Providence seemed to have marked the wrong boy."

The story is not exactly to the point of anything, only it recurred to me while I was thinking over the Farnborough schools, as being somehow characteristic of them. They were such odd affairs, those schools; it puzzles me to understand why they were ever started, or why any reasonable man or woman ever sent a child to them. Yet there they were, forerunners of Education (with a capital E), and they should be commemorated. I sometimes wonder if they really had as much effect on village life as did the example and influence of people like Mrs. Clayton; more likely, by some subtler growth of the human spirit, the village life itself was getting ready for both influences—for examples in taste from the lady and for conscious instruction at school too. Anyhow, the population supported schools. Farmer Smith's wife may have reasoned that education was a mistake. I remember hearing her, in the seventies, protest that it would set people above their station; but she never dreamt of standing out from the prevailing movement, forty years earlier. Had she not helped her husband learn to read and write? Did she not accept Mrs. Cooke, albeit schoolmistress of the parish, for her intimate friend? One after another she sent her young family to this or that village school—Mrs. Cooke's or another. Certainly she did not, then, disapprove of education; and the children, I have reason to believe, appreciated in after years their advantages from it. The testimony is Ann's and John's solely. They by no means pretended to have been brilliant scholars; but I think they knew how great a help to them even so little learning as theirs had been.

Why do I think they knew? Because one member of the family (Susan, their eldest sister, whom they spoke of as of someone almost sacred) had all but missed schooling. She was still a little girl when her mother, overburdened with household work, had to give up almost all work because of persistent eczema in the palms of her hands. There was no help for it: Susan was obliged to stay at home from school and become her mother's drudge. And this is what Ann, when an old woman, said of her elder sister, then many years dead: "I often think of it. Poor Susie! She hardly had any childhood." Indeed, in after life she lamented her want of schooling. She could not spell; and only with the utmost difficulty could she be induced to write a letter.

In such schooldays as she had Mrs. Cooke's had not begun. She was sent to Sophie Wheatley's— "A regular dame school, only she was a Miss." One would have thought attendance mattered little. Yet once, when floods were out across the road, "Old Jack" was taken from his work at the pottery to wheel Susan to school in a wheelbarrow.

Very different, in reputation at any rate, was Mrs. Cooke's. According to one account, Mrs. Cooke's school was started by voluntary subscribers and then supported by Mrs. Morant; but I incline to think it happened the other way about; the voluntary subscriptions had to be found when the Morants had started the school. Such at least is the inference, from the notes of Ann Smith's chatter on the subject, which have been supplied to me by one of Ann's nieces. According to these notes, Mrs. Cooke opened the school under Mrs. Morant's auspices and was paid a salary of £30 a

year, and at one time, if it can be believed, she had
as many as sixty scholars and employed a
monitress. It was a mixed school: a form across
the room was all that separated girls from boys.

Of "lessons" the children were taught spelling,
reading, and arithmetic—not long division, though.
Presumably writing should be added to the list. In
the afternoons, while the girls were at needlework
(for the great house), the boys—or was it rather
the elder children?—were having lessons in
geography (perhaps in history too), Mr. Eckersell
often coming in to take the former subject.

What were Mrs. Cooke's diplomas? Oh, she
had been a lady's maid, probably for Mrs. Morant:
so, as may be supposed, she knew more than a thing
or two about deportment. In dress she was
"always exquisitely neat." Black was her wear.
On her head she wore a muslin cap, close-fitting
and tied under the chin, and velvet bands hung
down from it as far as to the throat frill, which
stood up stiff and white. Below the frill she had a
white kerchief; and over her shoulders a cape or
fichu of the same material as her dress.

No less formal than her dress, not to say starchy,
was her manner. Holding her hands crossed a
little below her waist she passed (I think "passed"
should be the word) solemnly round the school in
the morning, while the children curtseyed to her—
but surely not the boys? And so, with dignity

and down-looking face she took her place at the
desk on a low platform. Then she turned, faced
the school, rapped smartly on her desk with a cane,
called "Attention, children," and after prayers the
day's work began. Once a year this opening was
followed by a formula: "Do you know what day
this is, children? This is the glorious first of
June—Lord Howe's great victory." I cannot
find, and I am sorry, for I might then have learnt
a little more about it myself, that she ever explained
what victory she referred to, or what Lord Howe
had to do with it. She probably remembered all
about it herself. To think so across the generations takes one back to the emotions that ran
through England very long ago.

There was one morning, too, when Mrs. Cooke
began school with a pained address: "Children,
a very shocking thing has happened. Lord John
Russell has been murdered in his bed by his valet."*
She went on to talk at length of the wickedness
of the times; pointing out that this new crime was
the result of one indulged fault—covetousness.
Lest the children should miss the lesson after all,
they were set to learn a hymn—the metrical version of the Penitential Psalm. Ah! why wasn't
there a cinema? If only Lord Russell had been a
modern Premier of England, little village children

* The reference is no doubt to Lord William Russell, whose
murder in 1840 supplies a convenient date.

might have known enough about this affair without being plagued to learn a psalm.

But Mrs. Cooke was nothing if not orthodox. Following prayers came "Crossman's"—a text-book on the Church seasons; and, after that, the Church Catechism and another simpler catechism explanatory of it. On Ascension Day, and twice a week during Lent, she took her school to church. I have told how she had the children stand up when Mr. Morant walked up the church. I ought to have told also that, during prayers, they knelt on the seats, with their backs to the chancel. This gave them the privilege—but I think it was hardly designed for that, though there was a fine lesson in it — of facing the paupers at the back of the church after seeing the squire at the front.

Though nothing of the sort was hinted, it may be supposed that Mrs. Cooke's school amounted to a sort of unrecognized but real church choir. Besides the metrical version of the Psalms, ten or a dozen hymns were printed at the end of the Prayer-Books; and the instrumental accompaniment was provided by a barrel-organ or hurdy-gurdy prepared for about eight of Tate and Brady's tunes. In Mrs. Clayton's time some of the girls—and mightily proud of it they were—went to the rectory for singing practices, conducted by Mrs. Clayton; for she had a piano there. Scripture lessons too were given at the rectory by the rector's wife.

The usual punishment for boys was to stand them on forms—a thing that on certain occasions encouraged naughtiness, enabling the boys to see out of window. Less pleasant was it to be obliged to stand, palms upwards, holding up a Bible high on each hand. A rap on the elbow from Mrs. Cooke's cane was the reward of flinching. She punished a boy once by administering to him a dose of salts. Fools' caps were not unknown in the school. Sometimes (it's suggestive of David Copperfield) a card was hung round the little culprit's neck, bearing the name of this or that fault.

Appeals to the sense of shame seem to have entered largely into the idea of punishment: the " herd-instinct" of the other scholars was enlisted to cast ridicule on a fault. On occasion even cruelty was excited. Once Mr. Eckersell (it is the worst thing I ever heard of him) was fool enough to bring this to pass. A boy had been complaining of a sore hand and getting a deal of pity and indulgence from Mrs. Cooke on account of it. Then, to his undoing, came in Mr. Eckersell. The rector saw the wounded hand, sent for soap and water, and—soon washed the wound clean away. Great then was the rector's indignation. After lecturing the boy he called upon the other children to chase

him out of school and show him what they thought
of liars. Thereupon the children tumbled out pell-
mell, throwing stones at their prey and tripping
him up. It wasn't exactly a "public school"
exploit. But the rector began it. Mrs. Cooke's
attitude must have been interesting. Amongst the
children eager to persecute the luckless boy was little
Ann Smith, to whom, after it was over, Mrs. Cooke
expostulated, "Oh, Ann! I didn't think *you* would
have done that!"

Ann, so sensitive and conscientious in her old
age, and at that later period so considerate to all
other people, never pretended to have been a particularly good girl at school. Half penitent over
the memories of what she had done, she used to
twinkle with demure amusement as she told. "I'm
afraid," she said, "I was a very naughty girl. Not
a bit like your mother. She was one of the best
girls in the school, and a favourite with everybody.
Of course she was older than me. But I'm afraid
I was more bad by nature."

This confession followed the narrative of a mis-
demeanour, in which, certainly, Ann seems to have
tried to be as bad as she could. The first class had
done so well that Mr. Eckersell obtained a holiday
for them for the rest of the day. A monstrous
injustice! Ann Smith and a friend of hers—one
Matilda—told one another what they thought
about the rector.

Now there was a girl the schoolmistress called "Quick," because of her activity; and Quick, overhearing what had been said, and being a favourite, repeated it (surely not in all its horrid details?) to Mrs. Cooke; who thereupon stood the two small offenders on a form for the rest of the afternoon—a shame to all virtuous eyes. For Matilda had said something, "Oh, very bad indeed it was," about the rector. In fact, as I afterwards heard, she said he was "a bitch"; and Ann, not to be outdone, had given it as her opinion—the opinion of a seven-year-old—that he was "the biggest fool that ever lived."

Without any provocation from Mr. Eckersell a string of little fools—little empty-headed girls—got themselves into trouble one day by sheer silliness. Sitting in a row, and when their duty was to be at useful needlework, they sewed together the corners of their own pinafores. Had Mrs. Cooke been watching? When all was done, she called up the child in the middle—it was Ann—and then—— I know nothing more. No punishment was mentioned. Perhaps it was punishment enough to the little girls to be made to look extremely ridiculous.

But they were little and lighthearted. Never more lighthearted than in church that sorrowful day when Mr. Eckersell was preaching his farewell sermon. The church was crowded, and folk wept;

for he was "as kind a man as ever lived," and all loved him. But said Ann, with her penitent, mischievous smile and using strong emphasis, "I did have the most joyful afternoon imaginable. . . . For we school-children were packed away into a corner of the church; and we played. . . . Oh, it was delightful." For what was the schoolmistress at? Why, she was crying, like the rest of the grown-ups.

Poor Mrs. Cooke! Perhaps she needed a friend more than the most do. She had a husband, who had been first a weaver and then a sailor, but, from the opening of the school, lived at home. For an occupation, though it amounted to no more than a hobby, he baked bread for the great house. Sometimes, on his way to find something, he would come into the schoolroom; and any boy who stood in his way had a flick from the whip Mr. Cooke—I don't know why—carried with him. Certainly he was a hot-tempered man. He cannot have been an asset to the school; and it's likely that, with such a husband, his wife was particularly in need of a friend. She made a confidante of Mrs. Smith at Street Farm, to whom sometimes the children were charged with cryptic messages. "Give my love to your mother, my dear, and tell her the wind's in the north." The reference was to Mr. Cooke's stormy temper.

CHAPTER XIX

SCHOOLS

II.—Mrs. M——'s

MR. ECKERSELL left Farnborough in May, 1839. About 1840 the first railway train ran through Farnborough; and Mrs. Cooke must have been still carrying on her school then; for I have it on record that she took her schoolchildren (Ann Smith, then about nine years old, amongst them) to see the first train. But already the two older ones of Farmer Smith's children had done with school. Susan had finished with the Sophie Wheatleys of her day some five years earlier. William also, a couple of years younger than Susan, had probably begun work. He had been to Mr. Richardson's boys' school at Frimley for a time; and after that to the school which Mr. Taylor, notable "for scholarship," was running for Mr. Green. But the "great scrapes," which were all that Ann could remember about her brother's school exploits, were over at last. Ellen too was nearing the end of her schooling. Farmer Smith, in short, was half-way through the most expensive years with his family. There remained

now only Ann and John, and the youngest—Mary,
a toddling child—to be provided for.

Still, they had to be provided for. And when
Mrs. Cooke fell ill—somewhere in the early forties
—Mrs. Oliver, who took her place for a time, was
not so pleasing to the farmer and his wife as to
prevent their removing their children to another
school. Mrs. M——'s at Frimley was preferred—
a much less classy affair, and farther away too.

No doubt a friendship for Mrs. M—— herself told
in her favour. "Such a nice woman," she was
reported to me to have been—a little, short, very
thickset woman : one of the esteemed Watts family,
and one who had been to a boarding-school too.
Why should she not do well as schoolmistress?

And very likely the Smiths had compassion for
her also. Marrying beneath her, she had unques-
tionably fallen upon hard times. Every penny was
of importance to her. Besides keeping school, to
eke out a living she sold sweets, her scholars presumably looking on the while. It is a wonder
where money came from enough to encourage this
enterprise. But there was a Captain Abraham—
owner of Frimley Manor before the Burrells
bought it; husband, too, of Lady Palmer's daughter
Caroline—who, being a kindly gentleman, would
sometimes give children pennies to buy sweets;
and it's likely that Mrs. M—— was occasionally
the richer for Captain Abraham's pennies.

L

To look into her school would be to see into a cottage kitchen, fifteen feet square or so, not so big as the kitchen at Street Farm, but thick with children. Twenty or more of them there were, on three forms; but when Ann Smith came she was accommodated with a chair at the end of one of the forms. For besides being one of the oldest of the scholars, she was the biggest of them; could not do with the ordinary seating, and even at play with the others out of doors was ashamed of her size. How little the littlest were I cannot tell. But sometimes they went to sleep, and were sent out to the staircase to sleep their sleep in peace. Little ones like this being admitted, Ann had the pleasure at last of taking her own small sister to school; and very proud Ann felt of a charge so dainty as she thought Mary, and so clever. But, once at the school, Mary refused to open her lips; and eventually, when Mrs. Cooke resumed, went to Farnborough.

I cannot but think that, in this matter, Mary was wiser than her seniors. Mrs. M——'s was really no place for little children. Not only was the school carried on, and the sweetshop business too, in that kitchen. Here also—there was nowhere else—dinner was prepared for the cottage household. Always by the fire sat Mrs. M——'s mother—or perhaps it was her mother-in-law—a good old soul enough, very infirm and old; and one of the elder schoolgirls used to bring her the potatoes to peel or the peas to shell. Not such a bad thing, that, for girls at school. But in this case it was overdone. And there was a worse interruption still. Mr. Cooke's occasional brief invasions of his wife's school at Farnborough were nothing compared to the long disturbance of work at Frimley habitually caused by the husband's return to the cottage as part of his daily routine.

Even at the best—even had he been a presentable and helpful man—he must have been a hindrance in that kitchen. He was a postman; and in the course of his duties he brought home letters for sorting and stamping at the table under the kitchen window. And sometimes the schoolmistress had to help him at the stamping.

For he was far from being presentable or helpful. On his returning from his rounds (apparently he had a pony-cart) about dinner-time, his wife would question him where he had delivered a letter and had drink for it; and he would own to about four places; but his state gave ground for believing that he had been to many more places and had been "treated" at all of them. In this drunken condition he sat down to dinner—and then went to sleep, first laying a hazel switch across his knees. And during his sleep the nearest boy would be well advised to remove the switch if possible; for the postman had a nasty habit of waking up in a bad temper and thrashing a boy. He would sometimes throw his hat at an offending boy; a hard-glazed hat, probably of Captain Cuttle's kind.

As the children of the farm lived too far away to go home, they took their dinners to school with them, and maybe had more than their fair share of this postman's attentions. But I think their father's name and position shielded them from violence—even won them perhaps some savage sort of favour. John laughed to me once, recalling a kindness that had been shown him as a little boy at this school. The postman had had a mutton chop for dinner; had picked the bone clean; and then, maybe having gnawed it, handed it on as a delicacy to little John Smith, who, however, declined it.

School fees, it is interesting to note, were three-pence a week each for the two younger children, and sixpence for Ann. This difference, I think, was not because of her size, but because she was finishing her education and perhaps needed more attention.

What, then, did the children learn at that school? Indeed I do not know. I never heard of their learning anything, save that Ann, in her final course, copied out, if she didn't memorize, some pieces of poetry. One of them began, "Eliza stood to gaze o'er Minden Heights."

It has worked out so quite by accident; but I am glad that my tale of Mrs. M——'s efforts has come to that heroic note at the very end. Perhaps her soul hungered for this sort of thing, to support her through the troubles of her life.

CHAPTER XX

WORK AT THE FARMHOUSE

A CERTAIN Dr. Morton (principal of an upper-class preparatory school at Farnborough), calling at Street Farm with some of his boys, made a Latin quotation—"showing off, like," my informant said, though I don't know how she was to recognize it for Latin. Gentlemen, however, have been known to "show off." But in this case it was indiscreet. Farmer Smith's wife took Dr. Morton's meaning; whereat he exclaimed that he should have to take care how he talked, before her.

It is not to be supposed, from this, that Mrs. Smith had any Latin, or any other language but English; but the incident does suggest that in education, with her boarding-school training, she was always far ahead of her own family or of anybody else from the village schools. But this superiority of book-learning—it's to the credit of her boarding-school to say—by no means made her idle or helpless as a farmer's wife, manager of his home and mother of his family.

Part of her credit, none the less, should go to her own earlier home. Her mother must have been

MRS. SUSANNAH SMITH

a strenuous and an able woman—it cannot be doubted. Some of the things Susannah Smith was careful to do in the farmhouse at Farnborough were imitations of what she had seen done well while she was still Susannah Blackburn in the inn at Westminster. Where else can she have learnt to see that the glasses on the farm dresser were polished so well and set out so tastefully as to be remembered long afterwards with admiration? In those early years, before the grandeur of the horse-hair sofa had been introduced into the sitting-room—"the other room," as it was called—the dresser I afterwards knew at the back of the kitchen stood by the wall in the sitting-room. A white cloth was spread on it. Three decanters, one above the other, occupied the centre places on ledge and shelves; on either side were the glasses—plates too —set out symmetrically; and "they did shine so," Ann said. It's odd to me if all this orderliness was quite a new thing—if it did not mostly come from the home where Susannah Smith was brought up.

Where she was, housework went with a zest. And it must have involved hard scouring and scrubbing, probably with straw in place of a scrubbing-brush. Not yet had the day for carpets come to the farm-house. The oak floors were sprinkled with sand (where obtained I cannot guess: the immediate neighbourhood had none); and if the sand was dry it kept the boards very clean; but damp sand was uncomfortable. The brick floors at the back (scullery and dairy) were scrubbed out every Saturday—a performance Farmer Smith always detested. Yet it was gone through for all that; and very nice the bricks looked after they had been sluiced down (all the water had to be pumped: there were no taps) and finally wiped dry with a flannel.

Much of the apparatus that lightens the labour of the modern housewife was unknown in Street Farm while the farm children were still little. On the other hand, some of the distresses of modern housekeeping were avoided in that simple style of living. I have heard of no annual spring-cleaning, of no sweeping of chimneys; nor were there any grates to be polished. But then, neither was there any coal. The turf firing was brought in by the armful from the turf-house. Seldom, I suspect, was the hearth allowed to grow cold in the kitchen, where, as often as not, the capacious chimney was afire smoulderingly. Have I not, myself, known a lump of glowing soot fall on to the hearth, and heard someone observe nonchalantly, "Chimney's afire"? These trifles were regarded as trifles, where there was so much to do—where the farmer's wife herself was active year in year out at washing, mending and making clothes, cooking, scrubbing, making and attending to bed furniture, and a hundred and one other duties as insistent in her day as in ours. Little things we take for granted she had to provide for herself by her own industry. There was no such thing as switching on an electric light when the daylight departed. Tinder, matches, rushlight—all took time to be ignited, and all had to be prepared beforehand. So the preparation of these elementary conveniences became a part of the customary housework at Street Farm.

Of the matches I shall speak later. The tinder—well, I have already partly told this about it. Farmer Smith, failing to get his tinder alight, for all his blowing "Phoo-phoo" at a reluctant spark (think of it, on a cold winter night), would cry out testily in the dark, "Damn it, Susan, this tinder's damp," only to be told, "That it can't be. I only made it this morning." "Phoo! phoo! it's damp for all that!" The making of tinder — what modern housewife would know how much to make, or how to set about it at all?—was a duty to be sandwiched in regularly between the other jobs, and never neglected at the proper time.

Rushlights too had to be made, if only in small quantities. Composite candles were used only by "rather aristocratic" people, and even by these for ceremonious occasions chiefly. At Street Farm the main dependence was on tallow candles — so often needing to be snuffed. These, and even rush-dips, were shop commodities, but the rushlight, simplest of all, was a home-made thing. It wouldn't suffice Mrs. Smith for writing out her invoices of the pottery-ware. About eighteen inches long, it lasted only while anybody was undressing and getting into bed.

Yet need for this must have entailed on Mrs. Smith the making of rushlights, if not perhaps for herself, yet for the members of her household. I have never, indeed, made out who these were; and they cannot have been all at the farmhouse at the same time; but other members there certainly were besides the family itself. It was after Mr. Blackburn's death, and after his successor too. Two bedrooms and at least one downstairs room were available then. Meanwhile the farmer's multifarious business laid on him the need of employing more workpeople, some of whom slept under the farmer's roof. Two carters there were at one time—when the waggon was going to London twice a week. A boy—a waggoner's boy—has been mentioned to me; and there may have been others. And they all made work for Mrs. Smith, if only at getting food for them. Here came in a use for the benisons described in Chapter X. "There used to be eight to a dozen of 'em"—of benisons that is—"stood on a shelf at the end of the kitchen: they was kept washed every day and turned up ready for next morning." For this was the custom: every day a fire was going, to boil potatoes for the pigs. At the same fire skim milk was boiled, and the men off the farm (five was the number mentioned) would come in from their work, take down their benisons (with iron spoons provided too) and have hot skim milk out in the washhouse. They brought their own bread. When they had gone back to work, Susan and her sisters had the job of washing up the benisons and spoons.

An industry connected with pottery and farm too was the saving and preparation of feathers— mostly goose-feathers—for feather beds. I have told how Mr. Smith, as potter, found it necessary to give Christmas geese to various head clerks he had dealings with in London. It was really his wife who got the geese ready. About a dozen there were, reared on the farm no doubt; and there must have been a fine business over plucking them and packing them for sending away, each with a supply of onions, apples, and sage, for savoury stuffing. To picture the coming of this country produce into London dwellings is to get back into Dickens's days.

But the work the geese had involved was not then done with at the farm. Their feathers remained— heaped, to get a little dry, in one corner of that end room downstairs which was no longer old Blackburn's parlour and not yet Susan Smith's grocery shop. Here, until they were ready, the feathers remained; and then, with "Old Mother Parker" to help, Mrs. Smith with a sieve would sift all the dirt from them. Next, after being sorted, clipped, and picked over, they were baked dry and tied up in paper bags, to be ready, I suppose, for making up into feather beds. To some extent this economy was for purely family ends, the idea being (at a later period) to give a new feather bed to each of the sons and daughters at marriage. Feathers, however, had a market value and were sometimes sold. Indeed, they accumulated. Besides, chickens' feathers, though not so good, were now and then mixed with the goose-feathers; and so perhaps were those of pigeons. For pigeon-keeping was another of the farm economies. Mr. Green (who supported the boys' school) was very fond of pigeons. As soon as they were large enough to eat—when the feathers were just coming—he was ready to buy, and many were sold to him at a shilling apiece.

The baking of bread for the farm—a week's supply, the children helping—was done, as I have told, by the farmer's mother at the potshop cottage while the children were little; so that for a time the farmhouse was not encumbered with that industry. On the other hand butter-making was exacting enough. Sometimes Mrs. Smith rose very early in the morning—a serving wench with her—to make butter. If there was a superfluity, she salted some and pressed it into a pan; or occasionally—— But first let me tell of the serving girl. For this girl—"a big strapping girl . . . of uncouth manners"—seems to have thought the work at Street Farm sufficient.

She was cleaning the front windows one day (so the tale went, laughingly) when a stranger stopped, to ask, "Let's see, is this the Workhouse?"

"Yes," the girl said. "I'm damned if it's the playhouse, at any rate."

Yet she cannot have been a lazy girl. For occasionally, as I began to say, the superfluous butter was not salted, but was packed into a basket, which the servant girl carried off and sold at Barling's shop at Farnham, seven miles away. Not bad, for a walk—with a load too.

CHAPTER XXI

FURTHER ECONOMIES, AND THE SHOP

As I said before, John Smith rarely spoke of his father's farming—I don't know why. An expert himself, he may have found it too silly to talk to an outsider like me, and perhaps that accounts sufficiently for his reticence. Or perhaps it was true, as I have thought now and then, that his father, so good at the potting, was not quite so good, was in fact an amateur, at farming. Of course, as the years went by, a few details accumulated. I heard how the turf-ashes made so good a manure as to be worth any farmer's buying and sending for at seven shillings a waggonload. I heard about Mr. Clayton's experiment with mangold; how Mr. Callaway also tried and failed, by reason of neglecting his crop; and how at last Mr. Hutty, a Yorkshireman, managing a model farm for Squire Timm, showed Farmer Smith how to grow mangold, prescribing the manure, and the distances, and superintending the sowing on the ridges.

An experiment in sheep-farming also was once spoken of. The farmer's two sons, William and

John, had saved a little money, and were persuaded
by their father to put it into sheep; he thought it
would be such a good investment. But it wasn't.
The sheep got some disease or other and the money
was lost. Indeed, that is no sheep-country. Yet
Mr. Callaway, employing an expert shepherd, did
not amiss with sheep.

No other direct references to the farm came to
me; but indirectly I heard of other doings—heard
or inferred, as from the talk of butter one infers
that cows were kept. So too there was corn-
growing—at any rate threshing and winnowing.
One day, at her tea-table, where she had been
indulging pleasant memories, Ann exclaimed,
"How pretty it used to look in the barn, when the
men were threshing, to see the corn all up at one
side of the floor." She might have gone on, but
her brother John cut in with something about the
winnowing, which for many years was done with
"a fan." This thing was described—a frame something like a small towel-horse, with four fans (hori-
zontal, I gathered) on a spindle turned by wheel
and handle. From all this, with harvest suppers,
and other chance allusions, corn-growing may be
inferred; but, directly, it never was mentioned
to me.

The children, in their small way, were useful.
John said that, when he wanted to please his mother,
he would make some matches for her. Usually

they were bought, as will be told; for it's not to be supposed that John always yearned to please his mother. More systematic were Susan's duties—to be sure she was older. When calves were turned out to wean in the plat, it was her task (little Ann going with her) to feed them with skim milk. By the way, if Farmer Nash had a sheep that dropped two lambs, he would give Susan one of them for a pet, and this too she reared, just as she did the calves, from a bottle. How she went to help her grandmother at baking has been told. The art came in useful to her in later years.

The children were sent out, at times, to weed the garden—no choice flower-garden: it was quite utilitarian. Somewhere near the horsepond it stood, receiving the irrigating soakage from the pigsties near by. Onions, especially, Ann recalled attending to here, "spatting the ground down" hard with a spade.

Cheese was not made at Street Farm. A good store of it was kept at the back of the cupboard, that office, rather, which was partitioned off from one side of the kitchen (opposite the hearth there), and which Farmer Smith used to call his shop. I remember the place vaguely—the thin deal doorway into it, with slender brass drop-handle; the window which was really an end of the kitchen window; the sloping desk all along under the window, piled with seed catalogues (Sutton's especially, attractively coloured). I remember one or two knot-holes in the partition which you could put your eye to, and so see into the kitchen (if the bacon wasn't hanging on the other side); and also the primitive pencilled drawings of "dicky-birds" scribbled on the partition by an earlier generation of children. But best I remember the smell of cheese—two or three big round cheeses on a shelf at the back, with a cheese-taster (but I cannot tell where it was kept) somewhere handy. It was a small grievance of mine that I was not allowed to use this tool. But anyhow there was the cheese, deliciously fragrant.

Bread and cheese and beer probably made a large part of the farmhouse fare. Bread, this also deliciously fragrant all over the lower rooms, was plentiful. As for beer—it had to be fetched up from a cellar below the dairy. I remember that cellar too—or rather, I remember peeping into a horrible black cavern said to be the cellar stairs. Enter it I think I never did. But one of the farmer's daughters (Ellen, my mother, has been mentioned in this connection) was sent into the cellar every evening to draw beer for supper. The walls were clammy I have been told, and I cannot believe that, even on summer evenings, any good encouraging light struggled through the small grating at one end. In any case children disliked the place. Ann sometimes stood at the top of the stairs, while

M

Ellen, two years older, went down. I don't know that Ann ever responded to the occasional plea from below, "Come half-way down." Yet in her old age she was of the temper to do just that thing, from sheer kindness and sense of duty, and I should think it likely that in childhood she did not flinch. But the time came when this same cellar, when in short the whole house and farm, became almost subsidiary to Susan's shop; when that shop gave such impetus to the industry, not small before, of the whole family, that the farmer was sometimes jealous of its success.

But I must digress, to tell how success of his own had already laid a foundation for that of the shop. Though he was not much good with sheep, he was a don (if the word "don" may be used in such a connection) with pigs. To a certain extent it was easier in his day than in ours. No tiresome sanitary regulations interfered; no accursed difficulties about swine fever. Anybody might keep a pig anywhere; and, as I have pointed out in a former chapter, the Farnborough people lived up to their privileges.

Yet few had such opportunities as William Smith had. The farm that fed the pottery in one way fed pigs in another way, producing the potatoes and the buttermilk too which (under Farmer Smith) eventually became fat bacon to pay the rent. Much of the story of how this was brought to pass is, I own, disgustful. But one part of it was almost idyllic, as John related it.

His father, he said, would turn out sows into the plat, taking care only to stop all gaps in hedge or fence by which they might have got out; and there they were left to farrow—"loh, how sweet they did smell when they come in from there! Four or five days beforehand you'd see 'em—as if they knowed their time was near for lyin' in, as you may say—going about all over the plat gettin' grass together, until they'd got a heap as high as that armchair . . . under a tree, or against a bank—somewhere where there was a little shelter. And they'd come home smellin' as sweet. . . . But if you didn't get 'em durin' the first four or five days, the little pigs 'd be as wild as rabbits."

Of the further fate of such little pigs nothing is known; save that, thanks to buttermilk and potatoes, they became big pigs, fit to die. The potatoes were boiled in their coats in the wash-house copper by the same fire where the skim milk, as I have told, was boiled for the farm men; and to do this was usually, as I have also told, the work of the carter boy who lived in the house and went to London with the waggonload of pots. In this boy's absence the farmer's son William boiled the potatoes. At these times he loved to take out plates, pepper and salt, and butter, and enjoy a feast on his own account. I infer, from his having more than one plate, that sisters with him shared the feast.

Towards Lady Day, and at Michaelmas, Mr. Boseley of Yateley was sent for, to buy any pigs that were ready for sale—"a sty of pigs" being deemed worth enough for paying the rent. True, the pigs, feeding off the Lent corn and daily littered with the straw from it (else unsaleable), made manure of some value on the farm; but their chief worth was as rentpayers when sold to the Boseleys.

That the Boseleys would take them was a foregone conclusion. Sometimes, thinking them hardly fat enough, Mr. Boseley would say, "They're a bit pinky. Let 'em bide a fortnight. But you can have your rent." The day before they were moved a dung-heap was made up—with a slant, I suppose —and they were driven up it into the waggon by that route the next day. The whole transaction was marked by agreeable circumstances still to be told; but all these circumstances came to an inevitable end when at last Susan opened her shop at Farnborough. Though perhaps none noticed it, a piece of farm economy—almost peasant economy —changed them into commercial business. It is not to be wondered at if Farmer Smith sometimes grew jealous of the shop.

CHAPTER XXII

THE SHOP

ACCORDING to one account, old Blackburn, having lent £400 to his daughter Susanna at her marriage, and a similar sum on the similar occasion to his son Tom, left this money, in equal shares, to the eldest child of each marriage on coming of age. According to another account the legacies were to be paid at his death. I have no means of knowing which was right; but it doesn't matter much. Nor yet does it matter now what year he died in, though I wish I could verify a dim recollection that the farm children danced with joy at his death. It is possible that Susan had to wait until she was twenty-one for her legacy. Be that as it may, she went to London with her mother to receive it; was disappointed that it worked out to no more than £70 or £75; but with that sum for capital, opened her shop. If this money had to be found by her father, or if he had to explain how the original loan to him or his wife had dwindled to so small a sum, it would be easier to understand his jealousy of the shop; but, without that, the change of business involved, and the increase of work in his house, may easily have been irksome to him. Henceforth, not his own business alone, but his daughter's shop too, must have required his wife's help at accounts and invoices; henceforth also his two sons were not so much at his disposal in pottery and farm as to escape all claims from the shop. I don't for a minute suppose that, in that affectionate family, anything of the sort was hinted at or even thought; yet Farmer Smith may well have felt himself, again and again, put in a second place.

As if not enough work had previously occupied the farm family, bacon preparation was undertaken on a much larger scale. At those public slaughterings in the village street, under the "old pollard" elm, Street Farm became easily the worst offender. One needn't make too much of the nuisance; needn't see, in that "street," anything like the frequented thoroughfare it has become since the railway station was built there. It was but a byway. From the farmhouse windows was an unobstructed view right over "The Hatches"—the quiet meadows. For the village had practically ended at that point; beyond, there were but two or three houses, with their pigsties and turf houses adjacent. One side of the street, in fact, had but one cottage and one turf house—this last a mere roof supported on four posts. In short, the

"street" was less a highway than a common place
of resort for the Farnborough folk—a convenient
space for any purposes not so easily carried out at
home. Such a purpose was the killing of the
larger pigs—not the porkers. Four or five times
a week it happened, from October to April. Three
or four pigs in a week were sent from the farm to
keep the shop going: the rest of the village killed
perhaps as many more.

No squeamishness veiled anything, or mitigated
any of the disgust, of the whole noisome proceeding. The whole performance was gone through
under the "old pollard." Sometimes there would
be a tribe of children looking on; sometimes folk
passed by, indifferent. One special man was
always the butcher, "and if there was any curious,
slack, indolent persons about" (I quote John
Smith's words) "it served to interest them for a
time. They would come up and have a chat with
the man before he begun work; and estimate the
weight of the pig, or compare it with some other,
and then have a pull or two at their tobacco
perhaps, and so walk on."

The pigs were drawn out to the killing-place "by
a string." It was customary to spread straw under
and beside the killing stool; and as soon as the pig
was dead the straw was wrapped round it and set
fire to, for singeing the carcass. Afterwards
much water was used, but nothing else was done

to obviate the abomination of the blood flowing down the gutters.

In the cellar at the farmhouse were two brine-troughs ("trows" Ann called them, rhyming with "snows") for salting the flitches of bacon. A very disagreeable job this, which fell to the farmer's two sons. Salt they used—common salt and salt-petre rubbed in thick, for all but the gammons; but the gammons were cured with baysalt. Of those two boys at work by tallow-candle light—it's pleasant to think of them—of their village chatter; their cellar letting out a dim ray of light through its grating upwards into the night; their talk pausing at sound of some wayfarer going by, or at the creaking of the farm back door overhead (an incurable creak that door had; I have heard it, and I can imagine how it would set the boys listening).

The salting being done, the flitches were carried upstairs again, to be hung on the kitchen walls until dry enough to be laid in the rack under the ceiling. From there they were taken up to the bacon room, to be stored until wanted downstairs once more in the shop.

Gradually this bacon won a reputation that brought customers from miles away to buy it; and it may be judged that Farmer Smith's rent was more easily secured than ever. Once on a time the gammons had been set aside for one sure customer, whom Ann named "Mr. Smith from

London"—as if that might identify him; but that was no longer necessary. Susan, with her shop, had found a better way of helping her father pay his rent.

Still, I cannot help thinking that much was lost, if much had been gained, by the change. Apart from the advantages no profit can make up for, of peasant industry over commercial industry, Street Farm lost some agreeable social values when the intercourse with the Boseleys was given up.

CHAPTER XXIII

THE BOSELEYS AND OTHERS

THE Boseleys were a well-to-do family, whose name figures honourably in the parish records of Yateley. Aaron and Jonathan, and a third brother whose Christian name John Smith couldn't recall, were the pig-buyers who used to come to Street Farm. Aaron Boseley, "a tall, thin, old man," seems to have been the foremost of them. Such was his integrity that his statement of the weight of the pigs which had been sold to him was always accepted without question. His coming to the farm, alone or with his brothers, was an occasion of importance amounting almost to solemnity. The Boseleys were ceremoniously entertained. They conducted their bargaining with a dignity—or say a mutual neighbourly respect—very pleasant to imagine.

Pig-dealing was not the whole of the business. Complicated accounts on both sides had to be settled. For at Yateley the Boseleys kept a provision shop (even as Susan Smith was presently to do at Farnborough); and towards haymaking, and again towards harvest, Farmer Smith's own supplies being exhausted, he would journey to Yateley to buy "fat of the back." "Fat of the back" consisted of chunks of bacon—perhaps of the farmer's own rearing—"as long as this stick," said John Smith, showing his own walking-stick, and as much as eight inches deep, all fat without a glimpse of lean. Farmer Smith borrowed a cart, "one of these old square carts, like a raved cart," to bring it home in. For he wanted to be sure of enough. His haymakers or harvesters liked to buy it of him, when he paid them o' Saturdays. Perhaps, after the manner of the turfcutters as already described, they set their fat bacon atop of a dish of beans or cabbage, for the oil to soak down. Or perhaps they aimed to make thumb-pieces with it.

Sometimes Mrs. Smith herself went to Boseley's shop at Yateley, to buy groceries, taking one or other of the children with her. A treat this, Ann recalled. Quite a long visit was made of it—say noon till night. "The old grey horse" was put into the cart—'twas an impressive occasion. And the purchases made at these times came into the periodic settlements at Farnborough, when the groceries bought from the Boseleys had to be set against the pigs and the corn sold to them.

It was a nephew of the Boseleys who actually carted the pigs away. He was said to be wishful

to "court" Susan Smith. The families certainly
were on friendly terms. One of the Boseleys—
probably Aaron—once set off with Farmer Smith
to walk to Odiham, each bent on appealing against
his income-tax assessment. But half-way there,
Boseley felt such a pricking of conscience that he
turned back, leaving his friend to go on alone.
" He'd no conscience," spluttered John, with a burst
of amusement, " nor no income, for the matter of
that."

For all his lack of income and of conscience,
these friends of Farmer Smith thought highly of
him. It was said that Miss Boseley insisted on
giving him a horse and harness which her brothers
wanted to buy from her. She wished him to take a
four-wheeled trap too. But Farmer Smith
wouldn't have the trap. He left it behind, though
he took the horse and harness back to Farnborough.

In the absence of any explanation why he refused
the four-wheel it occurs to me, as one reason, that
possibly he thought it would be too pretentious for
a man in his position. People might have talked.
Was not one of his neighbours wont to drive to
Farnham behind a team made up with a bullock
behind a donkey? If this was good enough for
Farmer Nash, what should Farmer Smith be doing
with a four-wheel? Such a gift might have
brought him sorrow in the end. The horse, on the

contrary—"Old Dick" it was called, and he had it on condition of never parting with it—came in handy. My father's father built the farmer a light cart for it, and it was useful for driving to Farnham market.

Previous to this, a horse and cart for that purpose were hired from one Gregory, at Hawley. Duly notified, Gregory brought the conveyance to the farm; and in the evening he fetched it away again, his total charge being half a crown. Yes; and this was thought a rather extravagant indulgence. Evidently Mr. Smith had some reason to refuse the four-wheel Miss Boseley offered him. Sometimes Mrs. Smith also went to Farnham, shopping—chiefly drapery. She didn't go, indeed, until her husband had been able to save and put into her hands a substantial sum, to make the visit worth while. Her money was laid out at Hazell's shop; and at Hazell's she partook of the market dinner which the Farnham tradespeople always provided, treating favoured customers as guests, on market days. Truly, the day was regarded as a festival for miles around. There was no Aldershot; no running up to London. Farnham, queer little old town, was something of a metropolis for the whole neighbourhood, and its weekly market (on Thursdays) an occasion. On the Thursdays when nobody went to it from Street Farm, Farmer Smith used to say to his wife, "Get me a glass o' grog, Susan.   Must have it to-day.   It's Farnham market."

It was all the way from Farnham—seven miles—that a doctor had to be fetched—for a woman in travail, say.   Excepting for the stage coach there was no public conveyance.   People who couldn't run even to a bullock and donkey team could only get to the town on shanks's pony.   I have told how the servant wench from the farm sometimes carried new butter to Barling's shop in Farnham. Other people did similar things.   There was one "Lawrence Ruffle's father" (but I haven't the faintest idea who Lawrence Ruffle was) who dwelt at Cove.   When Smiths had the corn business in Castle Street at Farnham, this man would walk to their shop, carry home again on his back "a load of sacks" (that is, sacks for a load of wheat), and, having filled them, would return to Farnham—perhaps the next day—with a sample, to sell his wheat.   Certainly he was at no pains to follow the "turnpike" road.   Short cuts across the heath enabled him to go "straight as the crow flies," said John Smith.

This man, overworked perhaps, eventually lost his memory.   He used to say, "If they tells me what day of the week it is when I gets up, by breakfast time I've forgot."   And sometimes, on a Sunday, he would "put the horse into the shafts" and begin work.   His people would fetch him back.

Occasionally he had to be fetched back several times in the course of one Sunday morning. You see, there was no church at Cove, to keep a man's memory straight, showing Sunday different from other days.

The Kelseys were named to me—a yeoman family, who "owned a lot of land," and therefore were amongst those from whom Farmer Smith bought firing for his pottery, and, afterwards, for his daughter's bread oven. Boxing Day was their day for coming to the farmhouse for settling up accounts. They are mentioned here chiefly as indicating at how many points of the neighbourhood William Smith's daily business brought him into intimate touch with men and things. A "deal," and a settling up with the Kelseys; and that was all, with them. But the same sort of thing must have been going on all the time with one or another, all across the countryside.

Yet was life not all business, or all toil. It's true, no holidays, in the modern sense, came the way of these provincials. Much more than is possible with most of ourselves they got themselves into close intimacy with the details of their own countryside, its materials, its weather, "the lie of the land." This was their support; to be fitted close into their environment gave them "character"; they needed to know nothing that the arts could teach them about their country; and what should they do with holidays? I am not aware that I ever heard the word from any of Farmer Smith's family, until they were getting on in years and caught it from a younger generation. Suburban people want holidays; want art; but people like the Early Victorians of Farnborough I am writing of can get a closer delight in life in their own villages and by their own intelligence. Sometimes, like Lawrence Ruffle's father, they go a bit crazy about work; but it isn't inevitable. There are recreations.

The Street Farm family found recreation, not by going away from work so much as by welcoming the friendships that grew up with it. So greatly was this the case that their intercourse with one neighbouring family—the Kininments—became too ordinary and too pleasant even to be much spoken of in after years. The Kininments were always "on tap," so to speak. They were taken for granted. I was for ever hearing mention of them, yet it was rarely with circumstance enough to seem worth recording at the time. Now, when I want to tell about them, I find myself with nothing definite to tell. Chiefly they seem to have gone to parties at the Smiths', or to have entertained the Smiths, with others, at their own home. But it may be imagined that the conversation at those parties was always intensely interesting, being always the conversation of experts about their own business, their own work, their own parish.

Mr. Kininment (as I have already stated in Chapter XII.) was steward to Mr. Morant at Farnborough Park. A very able, practical man in a landowner's affairs no doubt he was. He must have been something of a wag also: a man of dry humour. It was told that Mr. Smith, having been bitten by Mr. Kininment's dog, pointedly sent Mr. Kininment a present of shots for the dog, which were politely administered on a piece of bread-and-butter. This indicates, as well as I am able, the sort of man the steward was—"Bob" Kininment, as he was familiarly called. In similar familiar manner, a Martha Kininment was spoken of—a daughter I think. For there was a family—a wife, besides several daughters and a son.

Mr. Kininment married a second time while he was at Farnborough, and the intercourse with the Smiths seems to have suffered a little. Probably it was always liveliest amongst the girls. The farmhouse this family dwelt in—"Sycamore," near to Mr. Morant's house—was often spoken of, and always with affection. It was near enough to Street Farm for intercourse with it to be frequent but never troublesome. A dim memory flits across my mind, as I write, of Ann mentioning how she stayed there some days. But I have no recorded allusion to such a visit. The name she always pronounced Sickymoor, and that is as likely as not to be correct—in reference to the adjacent heaths.

N

CHAPTER XXIV

"TREATS"

In the absence of holidays, "treats" bulked large in the memories of the old farm life. The chief of these, the red-letter day in Farnborough village, was the Club Anniversary. I have mentioned before how Mr. Eckersell, the rector, honoured the club feast at the Ship with his presence. Have I mentioned, before, that Mr. Smith was an honorary member of the society? or that the flags for the occasion, bearing the legend "Farnborough Benefit Club," were kept at his farmhouse from year to year?

The children's appreciation of this festival was measured by the "standings" that assembled for it near the Ship. No swinging-boats or roundabouts came; but there were "show carts," and with the show carts Aunt Sallys, and booths, or "standings," for the sale of gingerbread, knick-knacks, toys. Children thought it a great thing to go "to the Club" and count these standings. If there were many they reckoned it "a good club."

Of especial interest was a standing kept by "Dame Roberts." Dame Roberts was an old woman from the Sycamore district, where she dwelt in a solitary cottage right out on the common. Whence she got the things she sold at the Club I cannot imagine; it's hard even to guess what some of them were. What were "cuckoos"? Dame Roberts sold them; and there is no doubt they were suggestive of bird shape. But what they were for, or what they were made of, is not easy to surmise. I don't think they were gingerbread. Ann, in her old age, could tell nothing more helpful than that she didn't think there was any "composite" at that time. Did they even say "cuckoo," or do anything at all to justify their name? I cannot tell. The one sure point is that it was "the thing" amongst little Farnborough children to wonder at Dame Roberts's "cuckoos," wherefore Ann Smith wondered, doubtless with much satisfaction. The gingerbread at this same standing was stamped or moulded in shape of a coach, or a horse, or a cow. Sweets were to be had here too; and birds—birds on stands, with wire legs and real feathers. Still other commodities were wire rings, with a stone set in them—at a penny apiece. Enterprising Dame Roberts! If one could only know where her goods came from, who produced them, and under what conditions, what a deal of forgotten English life might be recovered.

Yes, the Club anniversary was a great affair. Then did Farmer Smith's children wear their best clothes—and the farmer his, no doubt, for going to the feast at the Ship. And then did the Kininments come to the farmhouse, to tea or perhaps to supper.

Tea or supper parties also were "a treat" in themselves, for days other than Club days. Always the same guests: the Kininments, Mr. and Mrs. Cooke, and Tom Watts of Cove. If there were others they were not mentioned to me. Perhaps summer evenings were sometimes chosen; yet, from the talk of the preparations, an impression has got hold of me that these gatherings were affairs of winter nights and snug shut-in candle-lit rooms and glowing fires. They knew how to make fires in Street Farm; nor did the want of coal trouble them. Not always could the pottery fires be raked out just at the right time; but always peat or turf was available (seven shillings a load for the ashes, you know, induced some people to keep a fire burning night and day through the winter); and we may be sure there was no stinting for the parties at the Smiths'. Four or five turfs stacked up on the hearth in the shape of a card house made a wonderful glowing fire, that smelt sweet too.

As for the entertainment—Ann said, "We'd have a piece of boiled beef for supper, and your grandmother would make tarts. . . . Why, bless you, it was a treat to stand by and see her making the cross-bar jamtarts," with the expectation of a party

—actually a party—to follow. Nay, it was a treat to go to Frimley and buy the lump sugar and the candles for the party. These might very likely have been bought across the road, at Bridger's, but "Goddard's at Frimley was where we dealt, you see."

Lump sugar—Ann had a rhyme, perhaps of this period:

> " We buys our sugar in lumps, in lumps;
> And sells it out in jigetty jumps."

Lump sugar, I began to say, was a great luxury. Long afterwards, when it was much cheaper, Mrs. Smith (helping in Susan's little grocery shop) thought customers culpably extravagant if they bought it freely. Yet she gave it herself to her guests.

The candles—"composite candles to go in the brass candlesticks and stand on the table"—cost as much as elevenpence a pound. A dainty used in the cakes for the parties was candied peel at one and fourpence a pound. It was usual too to have green tea, bought especially for the occasion at Frimley. The company played cards until supper-time. After supper they had songs; and the party broke up about midnight or a little earlier. Until this shocking hour the children were allowed to sit up. Ann, in her old age, had no memory of children coming to her own home. Yet children were present somewhere; probably at the "return parties" at the Kininments'.

Another "treat" once a year was the "Harvest Home," or supper rather. Instead of a Thanksgiving Service or Festival at the church, a feast was given by every substantial farmer to his men and friends, to which, as I said before, the rector was wont to go; and to which, it may be surmised, all the families looked forward as to a great event. At Street Farm the harvest supper was held (if that's the word) in the kitchen, with tables set— lengthwise down the middle. The fare provided consisted of two joints, one of which was a boiled leg of mutton; and after the joints came apple-tart and bread-and-cheese; the drink being beer.

Supper over, the tables were cleared, and the party, with their beer mugs, sat round singing until a late hour—perhaps midnight. Meanwhile the farm children sat in a row on the dresser at the back of the kitchen, looking on. As for the guests —the men's wives were present with their husbands, and the maids from Lady Palmer's were present too, these being probably smart young ladies in village eyes. At any rate they found the young men susceptible. Three young men were named to me as having fallen in love with one or other of Lady Palmer's maids at a harvest supper at Street Farm; and one, Farmer Smith's eldest son William, made a successful courtship of it. In some of the farms in the neighbourhood, but not in this one, there was dancing after supper.

Christmas brought other interests. Not yet had the Christmas tree been introduced. That, which appealed so much to my own childish cupidity and seemed, I vaguely felt, so venerable an antiquity, was a later innovation, I was at last shocked to find, and even the mumming was, perhaps, not quite indigenous. Instead of mumming, in Ann's childhood—say about the year 1840—dancers were wont to come to the farmhouse on Boxing Day: a party of eight men besides a fiddler, making two sets "for four-handed reels." I give the word Ann herself used—the same word she used for those dances in the bedroom her father sometimes fetched her out of bed for on his return from London; but I strongly suspect that the "reels" she spoke of were in fact morris dances, and that the eight men with a fiddle at Christmastime were following a tradition as old as the mummers' own.

There is, to be sure, another possible explanation of their dancing: Mr. Eckersell may have persuaded them into it. He seems to have looked upon his parish as a toy. He had once tried to revive a Maypole festival. Ann Smith herself had no recollection of this: only from her elder sister Ellen she had had some accounts of it. From hearsay she was able to talk of the Maypole; she could tell of the rector's rather excited efforts to egg on the dancers with a rhyme :

> " Turn your toes in, turn your toes out,
> Twist a little and turn a little,
> And shake yourself about."

Before Ann's time, however, this attempted revival broke down; but others may have held a little longer, and it is just possible that a fad of Mr. Eckersell's was the origin of the Christmas dancing. I have no means of finding out. The dancers were for the most part men out of the potshop; and their Boxing Day rounds probably paid them very well.

And as the pottery must have been closed, at least for that one day, there must have been in the village a joyful sense of escape from deadening routine into the unusual, which is in itself a festivity. All things were joyfully different at Street Farm at Christmas and on Boxing Day. The clattering dancers came and went. The Kelseys, as I have already mentioned, were due to square up their bills for the year. Men were due, too, for Christmas boxes. Even from Simmonds's, at Bourne Mill right away by Farnham, the two millers—Bateman their name was—turned up, expecting a friendly remembrance for Christmas. Had they not furnished quantities of flour for breadmaking?

It was a season of home festivity and commemoration. There was a turkey for dinner—a very large one always—the yearly gift from a Mr. Brown, who had once stayed at the farmhouse while recovering from an illness, and was remembered with pleasure for many years. More ceremonious, and better in that respect, was the feasting on toast and ale on Christmas Eve; a special thing, never made, never taken, at any other time.

The preparation of toast and ale was the farmer's own affair. With this ceremony the Christmas ale was inaugurated — good home-brewed, specially made and of special quality for this season. Hot, and well sugared, it was poured over the toast. . . . "The little old round table that stood in the kitchen" was got out, and the family sat round it to take this Christmas Eve fare. All, even the children, were expected to enjoy it—to enjoy it very much; though perhaps the farmer alone really cared for it. A touch of formality in the affair was perhaps attractive to him, as formality certainly was to his son John in after life. "He would have liked," I said to Ann when she was telling me, "your father would have liked all this, because . . ." "Because of the beer," she put in, to forestall me. "Perhaps," I laughed; "but more because of the ceremony." "Yes," she conceded. "He liked his little performance."

As it was for the master of a house to manage the toast and ale celebration of Christmas Eve, so it was for the mistress to broach the elderberry wine on the same day. This, so spicy; this elderberry wine, hot and with toast dipped in it, was a comforting and stimulating forenoon drink all through the winter thereafter.

These homely celebrations no doubt enhanced, and were enhanced by, a holiday feeling of festivity throughout the parish—a feeling itself sanctified a little by its connection with the church, its home perhaps. It is doubtful if this connection was really benefited at all by Mrs. Clayton's patronage—followed, since her date, by countless fashionable women in countless churches. Mrs. Clayton bought costly evergreens for Christmas church decorations and set them up—probably with her own hands. But already a simple village decoration was in vogue, with a half-forgotten symbolism, it may be, which still reached the village heart. "Old Bob Mason" the sexton, with his daughter, upheld a medieval tradition in this respect—knew what to do (because it always had been done) and when to do it. Therefore at Christmas he put up holly and ivy in the church, leaving them there until Candlemas. For Easter there was yew; what, for Whitsun, Ann didn't know, nor yet do I. It matters very little now. Probably old Bob Mason himself could not have told the meaning of these things; yet, until Mrs. Clayton interfered, Farnborough folk, seeing the holly in church at the appointed time, may well have felt as they would if some sacred and happy message was being passed on to them from their forefathers centuries ago.

The quiet winter twilights would have prepared their spirits. Sometimes the church grew so dark, old Mason had to light candles for finishing the afternoon service. Then (having already used clay for fixing some of his decorations) he placed his candles in little lumps of clay at the ends of the tall pews. For he earned his daily bread at Mr. Smith's potshop. So, when in after time I saw the Christmas tree lit with little candles stuck in clay on the floor, it's not unlikely the pretty show was really adapted from old Bob Mason's pious attentions at the church.

CHAPTER XXV

FAMILY LIFE

I.—*The Father*

FROM the simple church decorations a sort of austere gladness, it pleases me to fancy, conveyed itself into the family temper at Street Farm, without anybody there at all giving it a thought. Unawares, as the family went about their customary industries—so varied yet liable to be so dull—they would be influenced by recollection of the sober evergreen colours seen against the stone pillars of the church on Sundays. The Christmas holly and ivy, the Easter yew, would tell the same tale that the seasons told, of the onward movement of man's life; would give it significance too; would seem to repeat what had been felt about it by English folk for many centuries, thereby dignifying the otherwise insignificant-seeming moments, and encouraging cheerfulness instead of provoking a sigh. And so a tinge, a flush, of unobserved "colour" (it is no more than a fancy of my own) made it the less needful that the farm folk should have holidays, because the feeling referred to enhanced their daily routine, enriched it with impressions of the changing tides of life, set it against the half-luminous background of something momentous proceeding all the time in all men and women. Nothing definite makes me think this; but something of the sort seems to be required to explain the sober cheerfulness of the farmer's family as I knew them in after years, and also their happy memories of the old days, their frequent recollection of things otherwise too trivial to be remembered at all.

Certainly it was not all bubbling happiness. "We children," Ann reflected once, pensively, "when you come to think of it, we children were brought up in a very serious way." It was of her father's occasionally difficult temper that she was thinking. He gave way to tantrums at times, with provocation enough no doubt, or sometimes under the unreason following an overdose of ale or of gin and-water. Ann herself, never understanding such matters all her life, merely wondered, or on occasion laughed a little. She laughed, for instance, recalling—what perhaps she never saw—a minute of fierce anger between the farmer and his wife, at dinner. The wife had handed across the table a plate so hot that it burnt the husband's fingers. He, in sudden passion, threw it down, crash. Without a word, the wife passed him another, which promptly met the same fate. By this time her own temper was hot—or perhaps deadly cold. Plate after plate, until five or six were gone, was passed across the table, only to be sent smashing to the floor; tragedy seemed imminent; when the two burst out laughing at their own absurdity, and the situation was saved. But, with this temper, the farmer was a difficult man to please now and then. "I've been afraid of him," said Ann. "There, so we all was at times. We never knew. He'd fly into a passion all of a sudden, and we never knew why."

Once or twice, however, the immediate cause of an explosion of his temper was plain enough, and it looks as if his nerves must have been badly on edge, for things so small to upset him so grievously. Thus it was the having an iron spoon given to him for eating some milk pudding that fired him off one day. He was so disturbed on this occasion that he would hardly go on with his food. Another thing he found it hard to bear was his daughter Ann's habit, as a little girl, of giggling. He would break out in exasperation, "What the dooce are ye laughin' at? Silly! You looks like a idjot! If you can't behave better'n that, go and stay out in the shop." "Many a time," Ann said, "I've been in the shop for giggling." Again, as already mentioned, his wife had a habit of rubbing her fingertips pensively on the edge of her silk apron, or of the tablecloth. It was quite unconscious, and probably a symptom of worry. But it sometimes irritated her husband past all bearing, and he would

exclaim, "Damn it, Susan, can't you keep still!"
His swearing at the rooks in his fields on Sunday
morning was almost a weekly event at certain
seasons; and sometimes, on workdays, he would
swear at his men. It seems certain that he was
not always so temperate with drink as a wise man
should have been. But nothing worse has been
told of him than has been told in this book; and
much more might be told on the other side.

It is just possible that his family, very dull of
humour on some points although keen enough on
most, occasionally thought him angry when he was
only teasing them. Ann herself never saw a joke
where pain to others was involved. It only distressed her. So, in her old age, she still puzzled
at times what her father could have meant by his
apparently disparaging references to one or other
of them. Thus, of herself, "Ann?" he would say.
"Ah: she ent a bad sort. Terrible fond of
pudding." She continued at a loss, to her dying
day, to discover why he should have said such a
thing. In a similar way his daughters allowed
themselves to be distressed when, on a Sunday
morning, he threatened to go to church in his
"smocked frock," which hung on the kitchen door,
ready for his return. It was painful earnest to
them, and perhaps all the funnier to him therefore.

In speech, though he pronounced "oats" "wuts,"
he didn't say "gehet" for "gate," as a Cove-born

man might have done. Perhaps his wife's London taste corrected him. At any rate he was feeling his way towards more modern manners. That was a subject of admiration in his family afterwards. Poor in his boyhood, poor and hardworked—where can he have picked up the "delicacy" he showed in sundry little things? Nobody knew where; yet oddly fastidious he was on odd occasions. His pettishness at being furnished with an iron spoon was cited as one example of it. The iron offended his senses. Similarly, when turnip-greens were for dinner, he enjoined his wife to "get a new pipkin" from the pottery to cook them in. I have told this before. But why a new pipkin? That was never clear to me; but it probably points to some of the fastidiousness I have mentioned.

Certain words irked him, if used in what seemed to him the wrong place. "He liked you to give things their right names," Ann said. "If you meant 'jug' say 'jug,'" not "cup," as in Surrey. "He was very particular about that sort of thing." Nor would he have people called "out of their names." "We was 'Ann,' and 'William,' and 'John.' But such a man for making up words, when he couldn't find one to suit him." In reading aloud, a thing he seldom did, yet sometimes would do, from his Bible, he gave to *a* and *e* the sound of *ah* and *eh;* and since Ann recalled it, afterwards, as a curious thing, I infer that this was not his usual pronunciation. Perhaps he felt a greater simplicity and sincerity must be practised for the Bible.

He hated fortune-telling, which may have struck him as sinful. Yet a man so much in harmony with his neighbours could not but share their countrified beliefs. When his daughter Ellen went to have her warts charmed it must have been with his consent. Rumours, prognostics, forecasts, had their effect on him, it may be supposed, even as on others. Through his household, as through the whole village, the silly scares of his day went creeping, unchecked by Farmer Smith. It is not to be thought that he was proof against the consternation at the potato blight, as the tale went about that the plague was to be "three years in potatoes, three years in cattle, and three years in men." "Very frightened we children used to be," Ann said; but her father—was not he also uneasy? A kindlier forecast—one more of the many country superstitions about the moon—added an interest to the Christmas weather. "Light Christmas, light wheatsheaves," ran the old prognostication; but a dark Christmas, with moonless nights, "is prophetic of a good harvest. That's what they always used to say."

No doubt Farmer Smith always used to say it, as such things are said at every season by country-

O

folk; not, it may be, because they are conspicuously true, although they are never questioned, but rather because merely to say what others are felt to be saying is a help to a solitary countryman, as he gets up in the morning and sets about his daily routine, in his fields and his unchanging home places, wanting friendship.

These things do to say, too, when you meet an acquaintance. They put you *en rapport* with him; will start a conversation; will lead up to anecdotes. I make no doubt country lore of this sort figured largely and was the basis of harmony at those parties the Smiths went to or when they entertained friends. It may have been after an evening spent in pleasant country talk on this footing that a memorable walk home was taken, from the Kininments'— memorable because of the great sense of family happiness and family affection that lay upon the little party going home through the silent night. For a little while the crowding details of their daily doings slipped away from Farmer Smith and his wife—"really, they were as happy a couple as you could wish to see!" Ann exclaimed in fond recollection—and the interests of the children were to the fore in the starlight of that walk home. So Ann remembered it, with some emotion, for seventy years. She, with Susan, Ellen, and William, made up the party; and they chattered—chattered of Spring-heeled Jack, for one thrilling subject.

From the hill at Sycamore they could see lights far away at Blackwater, "and I remember father, saying," Ann told, "he thought it must be the vapour over the pond."

A further slight touch to the farmer's character was added when Ann told of the cat, Toby by name, who used always to go with him o' summer mornings, when he arose very early and went out to see that his kiln was burning properly. Very proud was he of this friendship; and one can picture him; or rather one can picture the cat, tail erect, purring round the master's legs, on his duty those summer mornings.

CHAPTER XXVI

FAMILY LIFE

II.—The Children

ALTHOUGH Mrs. Smith, it was said, must sometimes have wondered what next her husband would be at in his more frolicsome moods, and although the whole family were afraid of him in his outbursts of sudden anger, he seems to have had the gift of making people extremely happy as a rule. Indeed, this must have been so. One felt the reflection of happiness descending upon one, hearing his children dwell so fondly on the recollections of their childhood. Their father was of a friendly disposition, keen to enjoy other people's enjoyment.

There used to be poor little starved-looking boys employed at rook-scaring; and when Farmer Smith came in sight they would run about shouting and waving their arms to make him think they were thorough at their work. But they liked pleasing him. Several times a week he would take the boys home with him and give them dinner; in consequence of which there were always plenty of boys eager to go rook-scaring for Farmer Smith.

He may have remembered his own poverty-stricken boyhood. But I think he liked boys for their own sake, being himself still something of a boy at heart, something of a child. To his own children he was often delightful. One remembers his getting them out of bed on summer evenings to dance "reels" with him. Even more exciting, more delicious, was his occasional "calling for" them at school. One of his fields sloped down to the roadside (tall elms stood there when I saw it) immediately opposite to Mrs. Cooke's; and there were afternoons when, descending the field, he crossed the road and entered the school. Then after friendly greetings, he would ask the schoolmistress, "D'ye happen to have any little children here by the name o' Smith?" Mrs. Cooke would feign to consider a moment, but answer obligingly, "I fancy perhaps we have," and so scrutinize her classes to ascertain. Three little children of the name of Smith meanwhile—Ellen, Ann, who told me, and John—sat shy, almost frightened perhaps, yet dancing-eyed with admiration and excitement; until at last they were discovered and allowed to go home with their father before schooltime was properly over for the day.

At home what did they do? They had next to no toys. That balancing horse-soldier I have described—Mr. Eckersell at his departure gave it to the little boy John—was never a thing to play with, but a wonder to watch and to cherish with great care. There was a doll also—Ann won it for a school prize, and for years it fed the pride of the family, where it sat lodged up, plain for all folk to see, on a corner of a mirror in " the other room." Perhaps Mary, the youngest and the darling of the family, had it to play with at last. I remember seeing the grimy stump of a large Dutch doll dragged out from the floor of a cupboard, and its condition was a sign of rough handling. I have also seen a three-legged wooden elephant, named " Old Kimpety," which seemed to have belonged to a Noah's ark. But I have no other evidence that toys of any description were ever seen by Farmer Smith's children; excepting only—if it is an exception—a certain little waggon or go-cart I have mentioned before. This also the departing Mr. Eckersell had presented to his small friend John Smith; and with this John and his sisters—perhaps his elder brother William too—had much fun. Yet the fun was not so much in the way of imagination as of romping. The go-cart was even useful. Did not the children carry on it the flour and the bread between their own home and their grandmother's oven at the potshop cottage? The same vehicle provided opportunity for splendid romps. A little four-wheeled truck it was, turning easily, the two front wheels being on a " bogy " or fore-carriage. The youngsters dragged it up to the farther side of the gently sloping plat, beyond the granary; and

getting on there, let themselves go, until soon the
go-cart turned over and shot them out in a squeal-
ing and jubilant heap on the grass.

The end room, afterwards the shop, served for a
play-room in bad weather; yet I hardly see how the
chances for that ever can have amounted to much,
that same room having been let to Mr. Blackburn
or other lodgers, or used for storing goose-
feathers. But indoors the children were probably
given household jobs to amuse them. Some of
these, in fact, have already been mentioned. With
so much cooking, washing up, bed-making, fire-
making, their mother must often have been glad of
extra hands and feet to fetch and carry for her.
The children liked to watch her preparations for a
party, for a festival. Great was their gratification
if they were trusted to help—as Ann was trusted
once, when she had the duty (in the middle room,
that was) of turning the spit where the Christmas
turkey was aroasting. I think I have told of the
little iron socket for a spit at the centre of the
mantelpiece, under the old letter racks and the pair
of wedgwood vases and the china teapoy, but Ann's
simple apparatus was a worsted cord with knots
in it. But probably the chief pursuit of the children
indoors was chattering idleness. There were
hardly enough of them for concerted games, and
they had no home lessons.

Nor yet had they any books. One book their

mother read aloud to them; and their father too enjoyed it. "Esperanza" was its name: a very dull book it seemed to me when I tried it—South American adventures, of the "Swiss Family Robinson" kind. Yet it was appreciated at Street Farm; the farmer himself delighting especially in a description it gave of a fine cactus hedge. He was perhaps something of a connoisseur in hedges.

Meanwhile the comfort of the home fireside was in itself a joy. The coals raked out from the pottery kiln—Ann always wished for them to be brought home. Such beautiful coals! Particularly at Christmas they were appropriate. The children liked to see the ordinary turf fires, but the live coals from the kiln—glowing remnants of fires fed with whole faggots at a time—these were the thing! Sometimes, of a winter, the children would sit round the fire singing. On summer evenings they went to bed—the whole family went to bed—by daylight.

The children took a healthy interest in their daily food. Salt butter was a treat to them—they wearied of the fresh. Similarly they delighted in baker's bread. Of the home bread, truly, a week's supply at once was baked, and by Saturday all longed for new. Baker's bread, therefore, was rather a luxury: shop-bread and cheese—that was a feast in itself. During the winter they had chance to weary of almost every form and kind of pig-meat: hogs' puddings, gammons, chitterlings, souse, salted spareribs—they knew all the varieties, and welcomed any change. Mutton they almost never tasted; but sometimes they had a calf's head; sometimes even, though less often, a joint of veal.

There was a man named Cottrell, of Frimley. Two or three times a year he would come and buy a calf to kill. If he hadn't the ready money, Farmer Smith was supplied with a joint on account: sometimes payment was so slow that two joints were had. In any case the farm children rejoiced to see Mr. Cottrell come for a calf; it seemed to promise a welcome change of diet. In these circumstances the annual dishes were of course "a treat." Of the Christmas turkey I have already told. At Michaelmas—not necessarily on Michaelmas Day, but on a near Sunday (it was always on a Sunday)—they had a goose, always preceded by a "dripping pudding," a pudding of batter, served hot, in slices steeped in the goose dripping. "So nice," Ann laughed, that her mouth watered to think of it, still at seventy-six years old. As she was careful to say, the bread oven at the farmhouse gave exceptional opportunity for baking a goose deliciously.

Tall and big the children grew on their usually simple fare, "ever so much bigger (at fourteen) than I am now," said Ann in her old age, adding that she used to be "so ashamed" of being so big.

Were they, then, merely big and bacon-fed? They had no music—unless their untutored singing round the fire o' winter nights amounted to a sort of folk-music, which is very doubtful. Books they had none, art none; a tedious needlework was the best outlet, and then for the girls only, in that direction. There was no theatre to go to, or picture palace, or even lecture or concert. Village institutes did not exist. Nor did the farm folk take even any interest in bric-à-brac. It is maddening to think of their chances and how they neglected them all. What became of that piece of needlework —"The Queen of Sheba," reputed even then "very old," even then when it hung in the grandmother's cottage? Or what of those two pewter plates (and what were they like?) sometimes borrowed by neighbours to weight down the eyelids of a corpse? Or of the curious pestle and mortar of brass, which long afterwards was remembered to have been one of the properties of Street Farm? These things are utterly lost; and it is wonderful that anything remains from those days, so indifferent were the Smiths to the values recognized to-day. A large china bowl (I think it is shown in the drawing of Mrs. Blackburn in her little sanctum at Westminster) was used for brewing Farmer Smith's punch. That wasn't often, certainly. Still, the bowl had to be washed and handled as it is not to-day. A china saucer, one of a set, served as a soapdish in the washhouse. At the tea-parties the candles and candlesticks were stood on a choice little Chippendale table, as if it were a common table, only meant to be used! In short, the Smiths showed no taste, no reverence, for any of the objects or any of the pastimes that are held essential in any modern home.

But it must be remembered that modern suburban life, even when it goes to dwell in the country, is hardly able to fit itself so closely to a country environment as farm folk of old had to do. People who know what the crops mean have small use for the interpretations of art: the country skill can tell its own venerable tales to them; the woods, the fields, the lanes, grow very dear. And the Smiths, by their upbringing and by dint of their industry, had all these advantages. What is hidden from the wiser and the more prudent they were able to see. I doubt if the loveliness of simple things was ever revealed to my own eyes, for instance, so joyously as it habitually was to theirs.

To two of the farm children at any rate—my own mother and Ann—but I will not try to say what I feel the home life must have been to them. Ann in her old age loved to tell of the beauties that enriched their childhood. She had no knowledge of botany or of any art. But what could science or art have done for her? Her spirit was reached direct, by country things. One time it was touched by holly berries, glistening in December sunshine. "I used to think it was so pretty," she exclaimed, recalling and describing a holly hedge in front of the paddock at the Kininments'. Other details were remembered; as, turkeys in the paddock, a shut-in footpath leading past the Kininments' farmhouse to Morant's mansion; but this holly hedge, with its gay berries, seemed to have planted itself permanently in her memory. "I can see it all, as vivid, now," she said, with a delight that must have been seventy years old.

Another time the touch came from roses. When Ann was a child there were no such choice garden roses as we have now. A deep red rose was a rarity; and such a rose in Mrs. Clayton's garden at the rectory was a wonder which the children made special journeys to see and to gloat over, with their childish exclamations.

But it was the wild flowers that called up the dearest recollections. Foxgloves reminded her that, in her old home at the farm, the fireplaces in summer were seldom decorated with anything more than an unkindled fire. But there were times—"I remember seeing foxgloves there. . . . Your mother and me used to bring home such shoals of 'em. They grew there in the bank at the upper side of the plat."

And again, in that bank, were there not hedge-roses? Each summer restored, in Ann's memory,

as if the years made no difference, the June roses
which she and my mother strayed to look at.
Especially there was one nook, a grassy, bloomy
nook, shut in on three sides by farmyard and
pottery and intervening road, and on the innermost
fourth side lovely with one rosebush bearing more
blushing flowers.

And farther in, away from the road, was a slope
of special charm, notable (it would seem) even in
those days for sweet woodland beauty. Bluebells
(wild hyacinths) grew there abundantly: bluebells
and primroses "on soft, mossy, leafy ground," as
Ann said. There was one large patch of bluebells,
she added, which "your mother and me used to go
and dig up and bring home to plant; . . . of course
they died, but still——" but still, in short, the whole
place was memorable for its mossy beauty.

Round and about on the farm the two girls used
to stroll, "because we were so near of an age," said
Ann, for hours at a time on Sundays. They seldom
left the farm precincts, excepting to go to church
or to school, their father being averse to further
wandering. So they rambled—not on high-roads
or in public lanes; but through their father's fields
and across the pastures and along beside the hedgerows.

CHAPTER XXVII

MACHINERY RIOTS

So rarely in their talk did John or Ann Smith refer to the poor that it came to me almost as a surprise when at last I realized how little they ever thought of themselves or of their family as belonging to that class. They had reason for reticence, I see now. They did not choose to hear me disputing, as I might have done, a social arrangement which, they themselves never doubted, had been decreed by God's own wisdom. As they held it an impiety to complain of the weather, so of poverty. They gave little opening to speak of it, and though not uncompassionate, they never dreamt of trying to abolish it. Consequently, although Farnborough must have been, like Selborne in Gilbert White's time, "swarming with poor," such an idea of it did not enter my head for years.

It is true, I heard of labouring folk and of their derelict thatched cottages; yet the particulars conceded to me were by no means harrowing. That "fat of the back" supplied to the harvest men and women for food was not spoken of with disparagement. In terms almost of eulogy another dish furnished to harvest folk was described: a pale pudding with raisins in it, said to have been "sweet and nice." "Bless you," John Smith laughed, "'twasn't so bad as you might think," this living.

It is likely too that, the commons being still unenclosed, the poor had in fact not quite reached the pitch of destitution that came later. Firing at any rate they could get. Few were so poor but that they could keep a pig. All the labourers kept pigs, I was told. This circumstance in itself fostered some sociability: it was the fashion for each man to go round the village to inspect the pigs as at a cattle show. The labourers could even afford to entertain their friends. When any of them killed a pig, a neighbour might drop in at a mealtime and be welcome to a cut off the sparerib. How the forechine was preserved for a special occasion I have already told. No word reached me of unemployment. I got impression of a hard life—a life that had to be content, for instance, with rush-dips o' winter nights when people like those at the farm were burning tallow candles; but this seemed typical. The differences between labourers and their employers were differences of degree, rather than of kind. They were not humiliating. All folk had the same sort of schooling, the same sort of food and fire and pastimes, the same sort of clothes. In this last respect a curious kind of fashionableness even could be cultivated, to the extent of wearing smock frocks of the correct village colour—for the colours differed in different villages, it has been hinted to me. What need, then—I saw none—to discriminate classes in a population, where the only rich people were the squires and parsons, while a hard though cheerful living was the lot of all others?

Yet, to a keener wit, the occasional references to "Jack the Matchman" would alone have been enough to show that a happy peasantry was not quite the whole population of Farnborough and its neighbourhood. If the villages in that district had ever been Arcadian, they were so no more. The mere presence of the man I have named showed where class distinctions and destitution had found their way in.

Jack the Matchman (to give the information about him in the same order as I got it) was wont to call at the farmhouse once a week with hand-made matches for kindling at tinder-boxes. These matches were slithers or spills, probably of fir, dipped in brimstone at each end, and tied up in bundles to be sold at six bundles for a penny. Ann, who spoke of the man as "Jack the Beggar," saw herself in memory as quite a little girl, going to the door with a penny to buy the matches, and perhaps to report what Jack said, for he "always had some queer saying or other." Upon my suggesting that he was hardly likely to get rich at his trade, "No," Ann's brother laughed. "Poor old chap, he used to get too drunk to grow rich." He was an Irishman; and he added to his small earnings by doing errands, such as meeting the coach and bringing home parcels from it. His home, or at least the place he lived at (Ann made this distinction) was at Bagshot.

For a long time I learnt but little more. The matches interested me more than the man. But at last further details came out, which put the man in his proper place and threw a rather new light on the social economy of Farnborough. It was John Smith who told me, he being then an old man, consciously nearing his end.

Jack the Matchman, it seems, was one of two sailors, who systematically "begged" the neighbourhood, having their definite rounds and almost their recognized days for calling. Only here and there did they call—at "the better class houses: Calloway's, Kininment's, Mrs. Cooke's, Mr. Green's, father's and mother's, and so on. The rest was very poor people." But the Smiths, as John distinctly said, held themselves to be "middle class."

And these two beggar men knew the difference. So, when the first Mrs. Kininment died, who had always been very kind to them, and a second Mrs. Kininment ventured one day to scold, Jack the Matchman took umbrage and "never went near the house after that." Yet food, and perhaps a few pence, were to be had at all these houses.

P

Each of these two men had his headquarters at an inn at the foot of the Jolly Farmer Hill at Bagshot. I haven't got the name of the inn. It was recognized as "a beggars' house," and provided cheap food and lodgings for folk on the road. None the less the village folk entrusted confidently their small commissions to Jack and his comrade. Thus, "if anybody wanted to send a watch to be mended" Jack the Matchman would be asked to take it along and to bring it back. If he took it to Bagshot— well, Bagshot was "a little Farnham then"; that is to say, it was a thriving little town on a main coach road, as yet free from railways.

Besides matches, the beggar men sold kettle-holders, of their own make probably; rough kettle-holders, with a braid round the edge and a loop for hanging up. You see, those were the days of open hearth fires, when the kettle hung over the fire, full in the flame or the smoke; wherefore "to have a kettle-holder on the hook was as necessary as to keep the fire alight."

There were also ballads. The word, pronounced "pallats" at first, puzzled me; and throughout it was said with *t* instead of *d* at the end. But there was no doubt what was meant. A ballad was "of thin tissue paper," with two songs printed on it; and I fancied that in John Smith's mind the whole thing—songs, paper, and all—made up one ballad. "Grown-up chaps" in particular prized the ballads, folding them up very carefully to carry away in their pockets. Very soon they learnt to sing the songs, adapting any tune, or perhaps an appropriate tune was suggested at the top of the verses. I asked whence these wares came into the sailor's hands, but could get no nearer to their source than Bagshot.

Wherever it may have been, there were beggars at Farnborough, besides very poor folk and a few middle-class houses. In fact the ancient class war was already smouldering there — even sputtering now and then into hottish sparks. There were riots. At any rate there was fear of them; their date about 1840 to 1846, as near as I can make out, though two or three years earlier would better fit some of the circumstances.

It is odd that my curiosity over this matter was first aroused by an old Farnham man, now dead. I knew that a "watchman's rattle"—a dreadfully screeching wooden instrument—was preserved at Farnborough; I knew too that machinery of any sort had been absent alike from the old farm and the old potshop. Mere conservative taste, I thought.

But one evening the old Farnham man already mentioned happened to speak of people long ago listening, with ear to ground, for the coming of "the rioters," and this being spoken of next day to Ann and her brother recalled these riots to both of them : "The Swing Riots or Machinery Riots," said John.

He himself, a very little boy then, remembered his father, on leaving for one of his periodical visits to London, uging his wife (John's mother) to give up everything there was in the house, in the event of an attack during his absence. Several other details were given; and amongst other things John mentioned that, less than a year ago, he had been employing a man whose father had been hanged at Odiham or near by for taking part in these riots.

Long afterwards the other details told then were pointed by further talk from Ann, at my supper table. It was this last circumstance that enabled her to make the talk realistic in one particular. Streaking her fingers over the white tablecloth, she told how threats had been written on the bridges and barns of the neighbourhood, especially over the Dean of Chichester's barns. Threats of arson, she said, and sometimes (she streaked her fingers over the tablecloth) smears of blood. The men who were the chief fountains of this ill-feeling were named, but need not be named here. And Ann recalled how her father would come home and say uneasily to her mother that so and so had been written up. What? She couldn't remember what. But these same men would sometimes call out insulting, menacing, "dreadful" things to people passing by them.

Farmer Smith, always apprehensive, was probably unduly frightened; yet he had one reason to be uneasy on his own score. One of the ringleaders was a man who had been sent to prison for stealing potatoes from him; and the farm family feared the man's release. He might take vengeance.

There were no police. Special constables (Mr. Smith amongst them and Mr. Eckersell the rector too) were sworn in; for in any district where there was this sort of trouble, "usually the clergyman would take the lead," joining "the farmers and respectable people . . . to patrol the parish. According to the parish and the district and the danger they would patrol the lanes by ones or twos; and if they wanted help there was the rattle for 'em to swing"—the watchman's wooden rattle, which must indeed have set up a terrifying scream, sounding across the night in such silent places.

John, who had himself seen the chalked-up threats, but, in his own words, was never anything but one of the "respectable people," by no means held that there was ever real excuse for the rioters. He was careful to explain that "a steady man" didn't have such a hard time of it, with his pig and the credit at a shop "a steady man" was sure to get. But all men were not steady, or at any rate contented. Certainly "some masters were harder" than others, and these might have their barns or ricks fired.

CHAPTER XXVIII

CHANGE

IF the class war did so little to shake Street Farm, the reason was partly because the life there was so provincial, was rooted so deep, I mean, in essential industry with the land, the cattle, the raw materials, the weather, of the neighbourhood. Neither art nor any luxuries were there to be disturbed. Without servants the farm people did so much of their own work, depended on themselves so much for their comforts, that the earlier shocks of social change hardly touched them. It was the same with other changes. The coming of the railways made no marked difference to Farmer Smith and his family. It's true, the main South-Western line cut his little farm asunder. He had to go round by road thereafter, to get from the lower fields to the upper ones, and all the compensation he got was for the crops actually destroyed, while he was allowed nothing for the inconvenience he suffered, or for the diminution of his acreage.

If this momentous change had involved the family in serious disaster, Ann—nine years old then—could hardly have failed to remark on it. Yet what she spoke of was the half-holiday, when all Mrs. Cooke's school went to see the first railway-train go through. She remembered the point of vantage the children occupied—in one of her father's fields, where some of his best pasture had already been destroyed and where a gravel pit for ballast began eating back into the land "like a wound." Somewhere near it was that place of sweet woodland beauty I have already spoken of; but Ann had little to say, presumably because there was not much to be said, about any serious harm to the farmer from the coming of the railway.

In fact, Mr. Smith felt it worst not as a farmer but as a potter. Business, as distinct from industry, had always been troublesome enough. There was a story—John had it by hearsay, having hardly been old enough to remember the incident himself—how a potter named Antrim, in an old place where now is the Alma inn, found himself in difficulties. So he called together his creditors; and when they had all assembled, he slipped out of the room and was never heard of again. There was no suggestion that he failed as a potter; business it was that was too much for him. And whatever the troubles in that earlier day may have been, they were increased by the railway. Doultons at Lambeth, nearer to a good market and producing a better ware, were already rubbing the Farnborough potters hard;

and with the railway close by, Doultons now had a further advantage in the matter of clay. William Smith felt their competition more and more.

Still, it was never so great as to disturb seriously the even tenor of his way. A change more inevitable than the coming of railways—a change that awaits the steadiest provincial as much as anybody in the suburbs—was coming over William Smith. Gently even there, though, it overtook him—even where the years were turning his boys and girls into men and women and making an old man of himself.

In the family growing up there were no gaps, or next to none, until Ann was apprenticed, at fourteen years old, to a dressmaker at Farnham. As she usually came home once a week, this hardly seemed any break in the family; and there was no other for years. William went into the pottery; John, who disliked potting, turned farmer, and I have no word of him for very long. It must have been during this period that that unlucky experiment in sheep-farming was tried, as already mentioned in Chapter XXI. The shepherd at Mr. Calloway's, afterwards known to me (with much liking) as Farmer James Baker, struck up a close friendship with William. "Two dry old sticks they were," Ann reflected, in laughing reminiscence. And an odd thing was told me, in connection with this friendship. James Baker was one of a little party of three, the others being the two William Smiths (father and son), who stood in the little courtyard in front of Street Farm late one summer evening, cheering. Ann skipped out of bed to find out what it was all about, so she told me, yet could no longer remember. Was it news of a royal birth? and had the coach brought it? She thought so; but no sure details could be recalled—nor anything to fix an approximate date. Whatever the occasion, it is pretty safe to assume that Farmer Smith's years had not quenched his high spirits: he still found life good to live. He could stand out, practically in the street, and cheer.

His good temper prevailed when his daughter Ellen became engaged to my father. The young man and the old were on first-class terms. "Father," said Ann, meaning her own father the potter—"Father did think a lot of him. He could take liberties that nobody else ever dared to. Of evenings Father used often to have to run out; and as soon as he was gone your father would slip into his chair—that three-cornered one they've got at Mytchett now. And when Father came back he wouldn't move. No! And Father would come up to him and flick at him with his handkerchief and say 'Dash you, Frank!' He wouldn't have allowed anyone else to play such games with him, but with Frank—I believe he'd have been disappointed if he hadn't done it."

The farmer found too, in his future son-in-law, a willing listener to the old tales and anecdotes he (like his son John after him) was fond of telling over and over—tales of local fairies and witches, anecdotes of an England old even in his days; and it was to that same source he owed also a pleasure almost unknown in his life : the pleasure to be had of a book.

For a book was sent over from Farnham (probably Ann from her apprenticeship was the bearer)—a book entitled " Now and Then." It told of a poor man's (an impoverished man's) troubles, falsely acccused of murder but in the end acquitted. At six o'clock one evening Mrs. Smith began reading it aloud, and her husband " seemed fascinated " by it. They sat up reading until it was finished, at midnight, Ann also sitting up.

After Ellen's marriage not much other change came into Farmer Smith's life, until William's marriage, five years later. It took William no farther from home than a cottage near the pottery. At the outbreak of war (the Crimean War, I suppose) " the price of lead went up like fun, oh," but I never had reason to suppose that it made any appreciable difference. The neighbourhood was altering a little. The woods (fir woods) at Camberley were being cleared, John Smith, in charge of his father's horses, doing much of the carting. At Chobham a military camp of canvas tents was established just

before the war. It was a great treat to ride to
it in Bridger's bus, Ann said—"Cocky Bridger's"
her brother reminded her. But after the
Crimean War this camp was abandoned for
Aldershot, and the tents were replaced by wooden
huts.

Whether it was true, as I was told and have repeated, that Farmer Smith avoided Aldershot
merely from dislike of the change (the camp lay on
his road to Farnham market; but he was growing
old, with only two more years to live)—whether this
was so, or whatever the reason for his avoidance of
the camp, his dislike of it hardly extended to the
soldiers. Had he some special fellow-feeling for
them? There was a story—so vague in all details
I haven't thought it worth trying to "place" in my
account of his life—that he once had to pay "£40 or
£50 to a substitute to escape the press-gang"—the
militia perhaps. Some memory of this kind may
have quickened his feelings for deserters from the
uniform. "The soldiers knew him," John said.
"In the morning you'd see an escort goin' to the
station (the South-Eastern) with their weapons all
drawn; and about four o'clock in the afternoon
they'd come back with the deserter. Father used
to sit (for tea) where he could see right down to the
station. So, before they got up to the farm, he had
time to go out and cut a slice of cake; and he'd take
it out to 'em. . . . You see, he'd come out plump

upon 'em—they had to stop. And he'd pat the
feller on the back and say to him, 'There, be a good
lad. Don't ever do it again' ('ever be forsworn').
And how the officers used to laugh! . . . Well, he
was a funny-lookin' old figure, in his round frock.
And I dessay it made a pathetic sight, to see the
queer old chap, and this deserter puttin' up his
hands for the cake." John imitated the gesture
of a handcuffed man.

Three innovations are to be noted as belonging
to this later period. The word "whisky" was first
heard and that spirit was first tasted, by John, on the
day of his sister Ellen's wedding, in 1851. He had
journeyed a little—about a mile perhaps—with the
newly married pair on their way home to Farnham
(there was no honeymoon holiday); and then, leaving their conveyance, he had called on a Mr. Busby,
a superannuated butler of Mr. Morant's, living in
a cottage in Dogkennel Lane (next to Mrs.
Cooke's). To celebrate the wedding, Mr. Busby
brought out cake and whisky.

A little later than this, the first daily newspaper
in Farnborough began to be circulated. Farmer
Smith with a few others subscribed to it, and it was
delivered to one of them—Mr. Grimstead, station-
master at the South-Eastern station. The others
went every morning, to hear him read the news of
the day, and the farmer used to come back and retail
it, full of interest, to his wife. One item of news,

thus brought home, was of the Battle of the Alma, which sufficiently dates the affair.

Later still—it cannot have been earlier than 1857 —the first "Christmas tree" in the old farmhouse, and perhaps the first in the village, was instituted to please two of the old man's tiny granddaughters. A solitary branch, probably of fir, was fixed to a beam across the ceiling of the middle room: it was decorated with two dolls, a few oranges, and possibly some coloured paper. With some trepidation the farmer's daughters—grown-up young women now—awaited his opinion; for he had not been told and was by no means certain to like the new-fangled thing. It turned out, however, that he was hugely delighted—"thought it so pretty."

CHAPTER XXIX

DEATH

LITTLE by little the old farmhouse was growing more like I remember it. It seems the bunch of hops in "the other room," over the mirror on the chimney mantel, had been renewed there every year as long even as Ann could remember: her father liked to have them, "for luck," he was wont to say. So, every year, a fine bunch of hops was sent to him from Farnham. But in the matter of small adornments or comforts a few changes were gradually introduced into the quiet rooms.

I have told how the floors were at one time sanded. The first carpeting was a short strip, "about as wide as a bit of drugget," laid before the fireplace in the middle room. When, by and by, this was enlarged to a square, the family was very proud. This carpet reached as far as to the horsehair sofa of my recollection. The said horsehair sofa (I have a nasty suspicion that some piece of handsome old furniture had been exchanged for it) was itself viewed as a sort of acquisition. To make room for it, the dresser described on page 157 was shifted to the inner end of the kitchen, where it still stood

in my time, the sofa remaining against the wall in
"the other room."

Until the farmer's death the walls of the other
room were "coloured" a pale blue—distempered, I
suppose—and grew very shabby. He used to
laugh, "When I'm gone you'll be wantin' to paper
'em." And sure enough they did. It was the
farmer's son William who carried out the work,
his sisters helping. And fine fun they had, Ann
recalled—papering the ceiling too. Such a mess
as they got into! But they did it.

But before this, you see, William Smith's days
were done. It may be only a fancy of mine, yet I
have at least fancied that to his notion a man ought
not to slip into death until he had carried out the
full programme of living. Life should be gone
through, not so much from fear of dying but as a
duty, to be faithfully performed. Certainly it satisfied his sense of fitness to live "to the age of man,"
and by a fiction he achieved it, for he used to say
he was seventy though he never reached that age.
"Your father calls himself seventy," his wife remarked to Ann, "but he's only sixty-eight." That
was the tale of his years at his death.

For some twelve months weakness had been
growing upon him. He lost his appetite at the
same time that he drank more. At last gravel or
some other urinary trouble mastered him.

There was—there is, for I lately sat in it to try—

a little spindle-legged tall chair, meant for a child, but a favourite chair of William Smith's, although he was a big and heavy man. On his last day of getting about he had this chair moved into twenty places where he had been fond of sitting—out to the little grass plot behind the middle room, and into his old shop—twenty places at least. He would sit a little while and then anybody who chanced to be near (usually his daughter Susan) was asked to shift the chair to some other place. That night he went upstairs for the last time.

After this he lay ill about ten days. There had been—perhaps that same day—an expedition to the "wood field" at the farther side of the plat, but nothing could be got at about it, when I asked. The point was not worth pressing: it made Ann tearful after fifty years. During those ten days of his illness, his married daughter Ellen took to him her own infant daughter (who died soon after), whom he took into his arms and fondled, as he lay on his bed. Another time he insisted on having all the family around him, and a neighbour who happened to call just then was obliged to come and take a seat in the bedroom with the rest.

He died on the 2nd of April, 1858.